COPENHAGEN 2013

100 YEARS ON:
ORIGINS, INNOVATIONS AND CONTROVERSIES

PROCEEDINGS OF THE 19TH CONGRESS
OF THE INTERNATIONAL ASSOCIATION
FOR ANALYTICAL PSYCHOLOGY

Copenhagen 2013

100 Years On:
Origins, Innovations and Controversies

Proceedings of the 19th Congress
of the International Association
for Analytical Psychology

Edited by Emilija Kiehl

DAIMON
VERLAG

The articles in this publication (CD included) were compiled and edited to provide as true as possible a record of the Proceedings of the Nineteenth Congress of the IAAP held in Copenhagen in August 2013.

Cover illustration: Solvognen – Trundholm Sun Chariot, National Museum of Denmark in Copenhagen. The domesticated horse and the wheeled chariot were brand new innovations in the Bronze Age, when the sun, the wheel and the ship became central elements in the religion of the time. The Sun Chariot illustrates the idea of the sun being drawn on its eternal journey by a divine horse across the vault of the heavens by day and through the darkness of the underworld by night to be reborn to a new morning.

Copyright © 2014 by Daimon Verlag and the authors,
Am Klosterplatz, CH-8840 Einsiedeln, Switzerland.

ISBN 978-3-85630-755-4

Contents

List of IAAP Committees

Officers:

Joe Cambray, President
Tom Kelly, President Elect
Marianne Müller, Vice President
Jan Wiener, Vice President
Angela Connolly, Honorary Secretary

Executive Committee:

Misser Berg (DSAP)
Fred Borchardt (SAAJA)
Alessandra de Coro (AIPA)
JoAnn Culbert-Koehn (CGJILA)
George Hogenson (CSJA)
Denise Ramos (SBrPA)
Walter Boechat (AJB)
John Destian (AGAP)
Toshio Kawai (AJAJ)

Standing Committees

Ethics Committee:

Ann Casement (BJAA, JPA) Chair
Erel Shalit (IIJP) Honorary Secretary
Carole Beebe Tarantelli (CIPA)
Christopher Beach (NESJA/AGAP)
Christian Gaillard (SFPA)
Sonoko Toyoda (AJAJ, AGAP)

Congress Program Committee:

Robert Wimmer (DGAP) Chair
Joe Cambray (NESJA, JPA)
Tom Kelly (IRSJA, AGAP)
Angela Connolly (CIPA)
Marianne Müller (SGAP, AGAP)
Jan Wiener (SAP, BJAA)
Pilar Amezaga (SUPA)
François Martin-Vallas (SFPA)
Heyong Shen (IM-China)
David Tresan (CGJISF)
Caterina Vezzoli (CIPA)
Misser Berg (DSAP) Secretary to the Program Committee

Local Organizing Committee:

Misser Berg (DSAP) Chair
Henriette Heide-Joergensen (DSAP)
Elizabeth Kampmann (DSAP, AGAP)
Pia Skogemenn (DSAP)
Hanne Urhoej (DSAP)

Secretary to the President: Mariuccia Tresoldi

IAAP Secretariat: Yvonne Trueb

Editor's Note

Emilija Kiehl

My official appointment as Editor of this volume was meant to involve full editing only of the plenary presentations and checking that the break-out session papers were edited by the authors in accordance with the publication Guidelines. However, I found it difficult to resist delving into the task more deeply and the ensuing wave of lively communication with colleagues world-wide over many months after the Congress, kept me connected to the hub of the dynamic exchange of theoretical and clinical thinking that filled the Congress week. I am grateful to all authors for their prompt responses to my numerous emails and occasional requests for further work on their papers. The result is this volume of collaborative efforts to produce a faithful account of the abundantly creative and thought provoking encounter of Jungians from all the continents. I feel privileged to have had the task to read all the papers, often feeling moved, impressed, fascinated by the variety of angles and the depth of approach to the life of the psyche that our colleagues' presentations so vividly demonstrate.

As you, the reader, open and immerse yourself in this treasure chest of creativity, I hope that, guided by the images, sounds and colours contained in the thinking of our colleagues from different cultures, speaking different languages, living and working on different meridians, you will also find the pleasure, encouragement and inspiration to continue on our quest for an ever deeper and broader understanding of ourselves and of the world(s) we inhabit on our beautiful and deeply suffering planet.

The theme of the Congress, *100 Years on: Origins, Innovations and Controversies*, is present in every paper and I urge you to allow its spirit to accompany you in reading them. The clinical, historical, philosophical and social aspects of Jungian thinking that you will encounter on these pages make this volume an important witness, not only to the development of our art and science throughout its first century in existence, but also to the changes in the world during this period.

I would like to thank Robert Hinshaw and Robert Imhoff of Daimon Verlag for our collaboration and our warm, friendly, at times witty communications. My thanks also to Frederick, my husband, whose interest, help and support contribute steady supplies of energy and encouragement for my ventures into new territories.

Welcome

Joe Cambray
President, IAAP

Dear Friends and Colleagues,

A most warm welcome to all of you at this the 19th International Congress of the IAAP. What a joy it is to be in Copenhagen a venerable city with a long, illustrious past and a bright future. While heartfelt thanks will be offered in multiple ways to the many able hands that helped create this congress, including all of you in attendance, throughout this week, I wish now to acknowledge our gracious, industrious hosts, the organizing committee, and especially their chair, Misser Berg, for all they have done to make this event a most memorable reality.

Our theme for this week seeks psychological reflections on our origins, on our evolving history with its complexities, conflicts, and innovations, and perhaps even an imaginative visioning of our future. During the week I believe that you will find interest in Analytical Psychology to be quite alive and well in this second decade of the 21st century. New centers around the world have continued to emerge helping create a global dimension to our association while simultaneously regional identities have begun to coalesce, giving voice to unique ideas and approaches to be found within the diverse cultures making up our community.

This week we will have a chance to listen, to speak, to dialogue; to renew old friendships and forge new ones. It is an exciting moment to partake in, to help shape and be shaped by our engagements with one another. Without further ado let us proceed, thank you.

Introduction

Robert Wimmer

Dear colleagues, ladies and gentlemen, and dear friends, who came from all over the world to join in the attempt to take a look back on 100 years of Analytical Psychology, a look at what has been and what became, in years of decampment, enthusiasm, turmoil, disappointment, discoveries, depression, progresses, splits, (re-)unifications and drifting apart; a discovering together and steady growth in many fields.

After the Call for Papers had gone out the echo we received soon made it clear that a large number of members of our community is striving to fathom the world in a multitude of ways with various perspectives and an amazing plurality of applications of what in 100 years of Analytical Psychology emerged, came to mind, became ideas, theory, imagination, sometimes vision.

I admit that seeing this gave me a warm feeling of comfort because, to my understanding, one of the most valuable legacies we received from Carl Gustav Jung – passed to us by his writings but more by the personal example he gave us – is blooming here: meet your being, get involved, open your eyes towards the outer as well as towards the inner world, be prepared for all kinds of surprises especially for the possibility to find a part of yourself in the most unknown, become acquainted with the alien to find yourself, to find home.

Being presented with a vast number of proposals in the variety outlined above, it soon became clear that our look upon 100 years of our history would widely differ from any kind of statement of accounts or such. There is not even a red thread to lead one through swiftly. But with the joint efforts of the president of our Association, the members of the EC and the wonderful crew of the Program Committee, which I have the honor to chair, we discovered not only one red thread but a network of paths which sometimes, in the most unexpected ways, tie together the seemingly incohesive .

So, today you are invited to follow us in the exciting experience of exploring and bringing together the broad multitude of what has been and what is thought, felt, imagined and done in the Jungian world.

To further what can be, in my understanding the only purpose of this Congress – to meet in enjoyable dialogues of individuals – we decided to invent, or reinvent, the role of the Masters of Ceremonies, outlined by François Martin-Vallas in the Program you hold in your hands. The basic idea is to bring to the audience some subjective reflections about what is forthcoming in order to give a kind of intellectual as well as emotional keynote to the day. So, each morning, you will be welcomed by another one of my colleagues. Additionally we, Masters of Ceremonies as a group, will be with you during two breakout-sessions over the week where everyone is invited to share their impressions and ideas about what is happening.

Now the important moment has come to express my special gratitude for the outstanding work the members of the Program Committee have done. I mention them by name: Joe Cambray, President, Tom Kelly, President Elect, Marianne Müller, Vice President, Jan Wiener, Vice President, Angela Connolly, Honorary Secretary, Pilar Amezaga (SUPA) from Uruguay, François Martin-Vallas (SFPA) from France, Heyong Shen (IM) from China, David Tresan (CGJISF) from California, Caterina Vezzoli (CIPA) from Italy and last and with very special thanks, Misser Berg (DSAP) who, besides doing her task as Chair of the Organizing Committee, functioned as secretary to the Program Committee in an outstandingly meritorious way.

There is nothing more for me to do at this moment but to wish us all a good event and joyful time.

With this I pass the floor to President Elect, Tom Kelly.

Opening Address

Tom Kelly

President-Elect IAAP

It is a great honor and it is with great pleasure that I welcome you to the XIX International Congress of the IAAP. Since the last Congress in Montreal, a mere three years ago, there has been tremendous movement and activity in our Jungian community. Little did the Program Committee know when it met in February 2011 to deliberate on a theme for this Congress, how appropriate the topic chosen, "100 Years On: Origins, Innovations and Controversies", would ultimately turn out to be. This theme was meant to offer us "time for a pause", in the words of the American poet Alice Walker, a time to stop and to reflect on where we have come from, where we are and where we are heading as a collective. The logo for this conference, the Sun Chariot, which you can see at the local museum here in Copenhagen, illustrates well the theme of the endless journey of past, present and future as it depicts the mythical journey of the sun riding though the heavens by day and the darkness of the underworld by night to be reborn anew in the morning.

If we cast our attention to the past, a brief review of the history of analytical psychology will reveal how, a mere one hundred years ago, major events were unfolding in the infancy phase of psychoanalysis and depth psychology that would lead to a turbulent separation from Jung by Freud and the eventual formulation of a novel understanding of the unconscious based on a psychological crises and descent to the depths by Jung and the eventual differentiation of Analytical Psychology as a branch of depth psychology distinct from Psychoanalysis. The publication of "Symbols of Transformation" in September 1912 would bring to a head the conflict between these two great men and would lead Freud to write Jung a letter in January 1913 stating that he would no longer correspond with him, effectively terminating their friendship and professional relationship and thereby ostracizing Jung. In August 1913, almost exactly 100 years ago, Jung used the term "Analytical Psychology" rather than psychoanalysis for the first time in a lecture given in London. It is rather auspicious that we gather here in Copenhagen as a community to mark the centennial of the founding of the school of Analytical Psychology.

Jung's re-election as President of the IPA at the Congress in Munich in September 1913 would set the stage for political machinations that would eventually lead him to resign his position as editor of the Jahrbuch of the IPA in October of that same year. As we all know, these turbulent events would precipitate a major personal crisis for Jung and trigger his descent into the depths of the unconscious and the recording of his journey, his dark night of the soul, initially in the Black Books, and then in the Red Book.

Turning our attention more to the present, we can see that since that time, the various schools of depth psychology have become, in general, more open to one another, in part in response to curiosity about, interest in, and recognition of mutual value in diverse perspectives on the complex and multifaceted world of the unconscious, in part also in response to pressure on the profession from the outer world. The insistence on evidence-based research and the increasing pressure in many parts of the world for a quick-fix solution to complex psychological problems with an emphasis on short-term therapy and almost exclusive focus on pharmaceutical or cognitive behavioral approaches in treatment has impacted our profession in significant ways. In this era of information technology, where access to information is but a click of the computer away, interest in long-term inner work has waned in many parts of the world and this has effected the practice of many of our colleagues. Government laws regulating the title of psychotherapist impact significantly on the practice of our profession in some countries and, in some instances even exclude recognition of lay analysts. More encouragingly however, in a few other places, certification of the title of psychoanalyst, including those trained in the Jungian school, has been formally acknowledged and legally instated.

Overall however, the zeitgeist of our culture gives little credence to inner work over time, to the spiritual, to the transcendent and to the reality of the unconscious. Offering Jungian analysis in our de-sacralised world, which has also been deeply perturbed by a significant global economic crisis, has become a daunting challenge.

At the other end of the spectrum however, is the current research being done in the neurosciences that demonstrates the intimate connection between the physical, relational and intra-psychic dimensions in the development of the individual as well as the importance of metaphor and the imaginal in dealing with issues of trauma and dissociation. The response to the publication of the Red Book in 2009, which was made possible thanks to the funding provided by the Philemon Foundation, also stands in sharp contrast to this zeitgeist. While many in the field were skeptical of how this book would be received and frightened that it would trigger yet another wave of negative publicity concerning Jung and analytical psychology, no one was prepared for what actually transpired. The interest garnered by the

Red Book surprised everyone and surpassed by far all expectations. Despite the cost of this hefty volume, over 100,000 copies of the Red Book have been sold and it has been translated into nine languages. The smaller reader's edition of the Red Book is now available and has been translated into eleven languages. Exhibitions at museums in New York, Los Angeles, Zurich, Paris, Geneva, at the Library of Congress in Washington and, most recently, at the Biennale in Venice till November of this year, all further testify to the intense interest in the Red Book.

Is it not ironic that, despite the collective pressures for short-term work and for quick and simple answers to life's intricate conundrums, there is clearly still a significant interest in the mysterious and neb-ulous world of the unconscious and of the imaginal as described and depicted by Jung. This, I believe, is important for us to bear in mind as we begin our deliberations this week and as we cast our attention towards the future and question how and where we need to adapt to the currents of the zeitgeist and, perhaps more importantly, where we need to hold firm to what we believe despite the currents in the zeitgeist.

This week, with the gathering of the clan, we will have the oppor-tunity as a collective, to do what we do in our everyday work, that is, to reflect on the past, to make links to how the early history of Analytical Psychology continues to effect the present and to consider and imagine how we need to meet and respond to the challenges of the present in order to safeguard the unique contribution of Analytical Psychology for the future. You will be invited to reflect on various facets of our profession as a collective, on our origins, on our innovations and contributions to the field, and on controversies in the world of analytical and depth psychology. Morning yoga sessions will give space for expression of the body and the Social Dream sessions will provide a container for expression and sharing of images from the unconscious. The morning plenary sessions and afternoon breakout presentations will give us the opportunity for more in-depth discussion and exchange on the current hot topics of our profession and, the arts will be well represented in the film, theatre and musical presentations. The theme of our Congress, "100 Years On: Origins, Innovations and Controversies", provides an apt and appropriate frame for the containment of the presentations and discussions that will take place this week.

Copenhagen is a wonderful setting for our XIX International Con-gress and centennial celebration and, rather synchronistically, the last day of our Congress, Friday, also happens to be the 100th birthday of the Little Mermaid, whose statue sits in the harbor and which we will the opportunity to see at the Gala Dinner at the close of the congress.

On behalf of the membership, I would like to thank the members of our host society, the Danish Society for Analytical Psychology, for their warm and generous hospitality. I want to especially acknowledge and thank Misser Berg for her outstanding organizational skills and for the extraordinary amount of work she has put into the management of the minutia in the planning of this event for months in order to ensure the success of this Congress. She and her colleagues and members of the Organizing Committee, Pia Skogemann, Henriette Heide-Joergensen, Elisabeth Kampmann, and Hanne Urhoej, have done an outstanding and exemplary job. I also want to acknowledge and thank Robert Wimmer, Chair of the Program Committee, and the members of the Program Committee, for their care, attention and dedication to the content of the program over the past three years.

Finally, I wish you all an exciting week of intellectual stimulation, connections with old friends and colleagues, encounters with new colleagues and hopefully the establishment of new friendships.

And now, without further ado, I am pleased to give the podium to David Tresan, our Master of Ceremonies for the day, as we begin with the scientific portion of the XIX International Congress of the IAAP.

Tom Kelly
President-Elect IAAP

Monday, 19 August 2013

Introduction

David Tresan

Master of Ceremonies

(USA, CGJISF)

I speak to you as a member of the program committee that has chosen from over 250 papers the presentations of this week. My personal hope – I do not speak for the committee – was to sum up the century of Jungian thought from 1913 to the present and tie a ribbon around it like a beautiful flowering plant, so that we could say, this is how we grew over those years and what we have become. The over 250 papers refused such an easy coming together under one idea, and I had to laugh at my hubris for thinking they might. There was to be no centennial declaration.

Was this then to be another congress that featured 'diversity' or 'multiplicity,' like a politically-correctly-named elastic tarpaulin that could stretch to fit an infinite number of diverse subjects and presentations? My mind very much wanted not to court anomie by any name. This centennial gathering was too grand an opportunity not to strive for greater coherence of understanding.

And so, I had to change my thinking. This last century of Jungian thought – and you must understand I am talking about the ideas, the psychology, and philosophy that are our infrastructure, not the structure that is the IAAP – this last century is like a plant not to be encapsulated by a ribbon, but maybe more so, it is like a flowering tree that absorbs our minds and creative energies and in return gives us fruit to eat. This century can better be seen as the present earth in which our tree has been rooted, its vitality foretelling a need for repotting in larger vessels over time.

But what are the roots of this tree? It was Jung in the early years of his professional life through his self experiments so incredibly well conveyed in words that articulated and safeguarded the counter-enlightenment commitment to the reality of the subjective and the reality of the transcendent. Between these two poles, there has been energy enough to fuel all of our variations on that theme. We today play with our own genius and toil in the in-between of those poles, in the ground of our examined and sentient world. We dedicate our activity to the care of human beings and to the truth of the human condition, and at a meeting like this, we tell our stories and our discoveries.

I, for myself, am not dissatisfied with this understanding I had come to of what we had wrought in this congress although it comes close again to regaling the virtues of multiplicity. But this is not the end of this story. Shortly after returning home from the last organizing meeting in Feb 2012 in Copenhagen, as if by synchronicity, an unexpected gift was given me in the form of a paper I was asked to look at. It was a scientific paper that took up the one fecund area that Jung at the end of his life had not brought to ripe fruition. In the mid 1930s, Jung – ever the scientist dedicated to material reality as an ineluctable partner of mind – began to lean more towards realities of the mind alone. From this came first the notion of Self, then 10 years later, the psychoid realm, and finally Unus Mundus, truths that explain but cannot be directly supported by empirical evidence. These are products of pure inductive reasoning, also called metaphysics and perhaps like products of higher math whose truths can yet have no known worldly reality. The paper that came to me picks up exactly where Jung and Pauli left off when they died. It bespeaks a reality that comprehends and sublates the reality of these last 100 years and gives it further context. That's what's new, I saw, and it's too early to speak of it in any detail. We are unique, I think, in the present psychological world to have informed and capable others present who in the course of this congress will take up these beginnings much better than I can here.

For an entity, like the last century, to have a definition, one needs to have a next thing, like one needs a two to know what one is. From the future will lie the view from which in time these last 100 years can be better thought and known, but not yet. For the moment, we are simply having a feast in the orchard. Or so I think.

Jung's Quest for *Aurora Consurgens*

Aksel Haaning

(Roskilde University, Denmark)

Presentation of the Text Edition

My presentation this morning is in four sections. Each section consists of a number of questions I am working on. I would like to share with you some of these questions and my attempts at answering them. The focus will be on the fascinating text from the end of the thirteenth or the beginning of the fourteenth century entitled *Aurora consurgens*. The text dates from the European Middle Ages and is written in Medieval Latin, the professional language of the time. *It predates* the invention of the printing press, and hence the original versions of the text exist only in handwritten versions.

Today we know the text, because Jung at some point during the 1930's discovered its existence. He immediately, as I will argue, understood its possible significance to modern culture and mentality. Moreover, he decided that among numerous unknown and as yet unprinted texts, the *Aurora consurgens* merited printing. There is no doubt that precisely this text meant something special to Jung's professional work. Moreover, he was anxious to extract it from the dark middle Ages and bring it into modern daylight, so to speak. In this way Jung wants to ensure that the past contributes to the present – not just as an antiquated mode, but by potentially enhancing the present. The contents must be articulated – just like "old" music needs to be played in order to become real in the present.

The *Aurora* text is the third and the last volume of Jung's concluding scientific work, *Mysterium Coniunctionis*, originally published between 1955 and 1957. The front and title pages of the original German editions state that the work is completed in co-operation with Marie-Louise von Franz. (Unfortunately, in *The Collected Works* it is published only as an unnumbered *Companion Volume*).

However, *Aurora* was not to be a mere supplement. Marie-Louise von Franz undertook the comprehensive textual critique and the contextualization, which introduces the text to the thought paradigms of its day and age. In the context of the early and highly original works published by Jung in the 1950's, the actual publication of *Aurora consurgens* as an intact archaeological discovery, marks the end of Jung's many years of comprehensive research into hermetic philosophy, alchemy, and the philosophy of nature that characterizes alchemy, his main research focus since the early 1930s.

Marie-Louise von Franz had almost from the beginning of Jung's Alchemical quest been an important associate. Without exaggerating, you could say that the publication of *Aurora consurgens* is the crowning glory of Jung's work. In this perspective, it might be difficult to understand how so few scholars in Jungian Studies, as well as in the field of the history of philosophy and ideas, have taken an interest in the text.

Structure of the Talk

As mentioned earlier, I have four sections, four headings, and four questions. The first questions are:
- How and when did Jung discover the existence of the text?
- How did he find the actual handwritten document containing the text?

These are the first questions. Later we shall take a look at what the text *Aurora consurgens* actually is – and not least, what did Jung find *in* the text – or believed to have found in the text. On the basis of this knowledge, we might be able to answer the question: *When*, and not least, *why* he decided to publish precisely this text? I believe that particularly the latter two questions are closely connected. Their answers complement each other, as I would like to substantiate in the final section of my presentation. So, if we can begin by answering these, in fact quite simple questions, we might actually begin to understand what the text means as well as the significance of Von Franz and Jung's interpretations.

A Package on Jung's Doorstep

It is 1928. At this point, a package with a manuscript arrives on Jung's doorstep, dispatched by the German sinologist, Richard Wilhelm, who held chairs in sinology at universities in Germany. Today there is a "Richard Wilhelm Translation Centre" at the University of Bochum in Germany. The reason is that Wilhelm developed a specific sensitivity to the process of translation, i.e. an ability to apply empathy and *receptivity*, in reproducing a text in one's own language. This method was unique and well ahead of its time, and today it serves as a model for modern translation practice. Wilhelm's mode is characterized by the attitude that egalitarian dialogue is possible between cultures – an approach that radically opposed traditional Christian missionary work. Prior to working for the Mission, Wilhelm had studied literature and music, and he was at least as worried as Jung was about the state of the European culture. For Wilhelm, the solution was not the traditional Christian mission, but a modern dialogue between cultures – particularly a dialogue between contemporary knowledge and *past* knowledge. Can translation render the past understandable? This is a problem that *all* cultures need to address and solve. That's why Wilhelm's method of approach is modern.

Jung had met Richard Wilhelm some years earlier in Count Hermann Alexander Keyserling's (1880-1946) *Schule der Weisheit* in Darmstadt, where they both lectured.

At this point, Jung became interested in Wilhelm's translation of the *I Ching, the Book of Changes* and the psychology of this work. At the time, Quingdao was a German colony on the north eastern Chinese Pacific coast. This is where in the mid 1920's Wilhelm came into possession of a rare text on longevity. The text was from the Taoist school of thought, entitled *The Secret of the Golden Flower*. Wilhelm had been allowed access to a rare copy of the text, which was printed in Shanghai in 1920. The permission was given by one Lau Nai Süan who, during the Xinhai-revolution 1911-13, fled inland and brought some Taoist books along. When the translation was completed, the old Chinese, Nai Süan, died. Wilhelm translated it into German, and it was this translation that arrived in a package at Jung's home in Küsnacht in 1928. Wilhelm suggested that Jung should write a psychological commentary. This became "A European Commentary," a decisive key text in Jung's authorship, written during the winter of 1928-1929 and published alongside the text *The Secret of the Golden Flower* in November 1929. (CW 13 pars.1-84) Shortly after the publication, Wilhelm died from an infection contracted many years earlier. However, the flower was now planted in the European soil.

As mentioned earlier, Jung's commentary in *The Secret of the Golden Flower* divides his work chronologically into the first and the second half. His first book is from 1902 and his last is the essay "Approaching the Unconscious" (CW 18 pars. 416-607), completed in May 1961. In the middle we find Richard Wilhelm's translation and the "European Commentary," which is published in the autumn of 1929, when Jung is in the process of putting the work on *Liber Novus* aside. In the 1959 postscript, handwritten separately, a fictive future reader is addressed: "I worked in this book for sixteen years. My acquaintance with alchemy in 1930 took me away from it.

The beginning of the end came in 1928, when Wilhelm sent me the text of the "Golden Flower," an alchemical treatise. The contents of this book found their way into actuality and I could no longer continue working on it" (Shamdasani, 2012, p. 129). We shall now take a look at this actuality.

Opening a Closed Book: "Artis Auriferae"

The publication of *The Secret of the Golden Flower* and Jung's European commentary kindles Jung's interest in alchemy. This publication inspires a hope to find a European golden flower, which *exists* – as "Aurora consurgens", also called *aurea hora*; perhaps not a *golden flower*, but it is literally a "Golden Hour Rising."

While in the process of writing his European commentary, Jung asked an antiquarian bookseller in Munich to forward any European books on alchemy he came across. The first text Jung received was the collection *Artis Auriferae volumina duo*, printed in 1593. (The title means: "The Art of Bringing Forth Gold"). According to Jung, it stayed on his desk, more or less untouched, for two years – most likely 1929 to 1931. However, the moment Jung decided to abandon *Liber Novus*, *The Red Book*, he opened *Artis Auriferae*. It consists exclusively of alchemical treatises from the Middle Ages – Arabian treatises translated into Latin, as well as purely Latin texts.

During the Renaissance it was popular to publish these texts from the Middle Ages, the printing press having inspired a renewed interest in the past. The publisher, the printer Conrad Waldkirch, was a staunch believer in the reformed Lutheran faith and he briefly comments on the individual texts he puts to print. Soon Jung begins to pay attention to these short prefaces in italics. The revelation does not come on page 189, his last in *Liber Novus*, but it almost does! On page 183 in *Artis Auriferae,* Waldkirch writes that in the hand-written treatise printed on the following pages, there is another text with the same title – *Aurea hora* – "the Golden Hour", which he will not print.

As you might know, I am not a therapist. However, one does not need to be a therapist to understand that material that is not allowed to be spoken about and printed, material that, so to speak, must remain in the dark Middle Ages where it originated, *must* be interesting, even important and significant. Jung's interest did not diminish when Waldkirch, the printer, actually explained, or at least hinted vaguely, at a specific issue that made him decide *not* to publish the text. He states that the author seems to be a rather pious man. However, he, the unknown author of the Latin text, compares the mystery of the stone to mystery, death and resurrection of our Lord Christ. Moreover, he states that the secret of alchemy is hidden in the biblical writings, especially the Psalms and the *Song of Solomon*.

So, instead of Christ's death and resurrection, we have the mystery of the stone? What does this mean? Paganism disguised in the language of the Bible? A symbolic understanding rather than literal? At this point Jung's interest in alchemy must have been kindled. From the first moment, so to speak, Conrad Waldkirch, without knowing it, hands Jung the key to what fourteen years later will become the central chapter in *Psychology and Alchemy*: the important chapter V "The Lapis-Christ Parallel" (CW 12 pars. 447-515).

So, in this chapter, in Jung's interpretation, two eras meet: a subject, which in the age of the Reformation was considered heretical and unacceptable to religious persuasions, becomes in modernity an important part in the foundation of a science of the soul. "Things have changed," from past to present. But it is not a gift to relax upon. It means work to be done.

A Detective in London

Having put *Liber Novus* aside and opening *Artis Auriferae*, Jung discovers that there once existed a book on this enigmatic symbol, which likens the *lapis philosophorum* to Christ, and that this book was not allowed to be published. Nevertheless, it did at one point exist. Where could one find this manuscript? Where to begin? Like in a fairy tale: "Look where you are!" Just a few miles away, Jung makes inquiries at the Zentralbibliothek in Zürich, where the librarians in the manuscript department could inform him that there is actually a relatively unknown illustrated manuscript entitled *Aurora consurgens*, the so-called Codex Rhenovacensis 172. The manuscript is most likely from the fifteenth century and hails from a monastery in Rhinau. However, unfortunately, the text is incomplete; the entire first section is missing. Still, this information is a start. It shows that a manuscript tradition has existed, and this inspires hope that an intact text with the full wording might be found *in toto*.

Jung must have been a kind of a detective. According to Barbara Hannah's *Biographical Memoir*, Jung apparently loved to relax with detective stories, precisely because they were not real. However, the *Aurora*-hint does anything but relax him. On the contrary, he himself now becomes a kind of Sherlock Holmes, and since he is on the track by reading *Artis Auriferae*, his obsession soon takes him to London – not to Baker Street, but to the British Museum. So, in 1935 we find this detective in London, in the Library of the British Museum. At the end of September, Jung gives the well-known "Tavistock Lectures," (CW 18 pars. 1-415). In the discussion session after the second lecture, Jung explains how the interpretation of individual dreams can further an expansion of the understanding of themes and motifs by finding supplementary materials in the history of philosophy and religion. This is Jung's so-called amplification method, which he attempts to explain to the – judging by the text – somewhat conservative British psychiatrists. This is the formal context of Jung's visit to England and here he offers the cultural critique that characterizes his work in the 1930's:

We Europeans are not the only people on earth. We are just a peninsula of Asia, and on that continent there are old civilizations where people have trained their minds in introspective psychology for thousands of years, whereas we began with our psychology not even yesterday but only this morning. These peoples have an insight that is simply fabulous, and I had to study the Eastern things to understand certain facts of the unconscious. I had to go back to understand Oriental symbolism. ... I had to study not only Chinese and Hindu but Sanskrit literature and medieval Latin manuscripts which are not even known to specialists, so that one must go to the British Museum to find references ... (CW 18 par. 139).

In the mind game that Jung engages in with the skeptical Brits, Jung's example is a stroke of genius: the sources are located in the British Museum, in the heart of British high culture, but do they know their own past? As a psychiatrist, Jung must show the Brits aspects of their own culture, which they themselves are unable to see! Jung's references to Medieval Latin manuscripts, unknown even to the specialists, could only have been made once he realized that the philologists responsible for the manuscript collections in Zürich were unable to find other copies of the *Aurora consurgens* – most likely because they were not part of those collections. He had to do the work himself and found indications that the complete text exists. Moreover, he succeeded in finding a rare print in the British Museum. Here he found the first "references" that provided him with clues as to how and where to continue his search.

What Jung did find, is the only extant print from 1625. It is located in the British Museum, extremely rare, and Jung never succeeded in acquiring the book himself. It was published by Johannes Rhenanus and it has a very long Latin title. Our *Aurora sive Aurea Hora* is found in vol. II. However, there is a significant problem with the text of this particular print. In terms of the correct reconstruction of the text, this print cannot be used. The reason is that the many variations on the wording of the biblical texts in the print have been realigned with the *Vulgata*, the "correct" biblical quotations in the Latin version of the Bible.

These small but significant variations in the manuscript's many biblical quotations constitute a significant aspect of the text's specific nature, and they are a substantial part of the specific cognitive experience it describes. However, having found the printed version, Jung can now identify the treatise's so-called *incipit*, its first words, universally used to catalogue texts prior to the advent of the printing press.

Having the incipit from the print: *Venerunt mihi omnia bona* –makes it possible to begin to search for manuscripts in the catalogues!

1937: Jung at Yale University

The comment in the Tavistock Lectures is thus the first, if somewhat indirect, evidence that Jung is on the trail and looking specifically for *Aurora*-manuscripts. Before the year has gone by, he is in possession of a manuscript with the entire text, written in a clear and legible hand from the fifteenth century. It is located in the Bibliothèque Nationale in Paris, which houses one of the world's largest collections of medieval manuscripts.

The story of the *Aurora consurgens* – from Konrad Waldkirch's preface to the findings in the Bibliothèque Nationale – is told by Jung in his first outline of the historical studies in alchemy, the Eranos lectures in August in 1936. In the original version from the *Eranos-Jahrbuch* 1936 Jung mentions the *Aurora* in no less than ten instances. Moreover, he reveals that a complete manuscript exists in Paris. However, it was not found by Jung himself, it was found by his wife, Emma Rauschenberg Jung! My guess is that Jung's wife in the context of her work on the historical sources of the grail legends, of which several are located in the Bibliothèque Nationale in Paris, has looked for the *Aurora*. She has been able to do so because Jung on the basis of the print in London could give her the incipit, the first words, by which the text is registered in the old manuscript catalogues. Emma Jung's historical studies of the grail legends begin around 1930, at the same time that Jung takes up alchemical studies. However, the fact that the text is actually found by Emma Jung, is not mentioned by the diligent detective. As far as I am aware, the *Eranos-Jarhbuch* from 1936 is the only place where this is mentioned. In *Psychology and Alchemy*, which contains the Eranos presentation in a slightly expanded version, the focus is on the contents, and Jung mentions only Waldkirch's preface as the momentum which inspired his detective work.

The following year Jung applies the contents for the first time. In the three 1937 Yale University lectures on psychology and religion, later published under the same title, Jung quotes the recently dis-covered text. It is in the context of the discussion of the modern consciousness' ability to distinguish between what Jung calls dogmatic and natural symbols, that Jung addresses the significance of alchemy in relation to the symbols of the nature philosophy of antiquity and later the Christian religion's dominant symbols. Jung now claims – for the first time in front of an entirely academic public – to have made the astonishing discovery that alchemical philosophy, as represented in hundreds of forgotten and often controversial texts and images, is in fact a repository in which religious symbols from antiquity and early Christianity quite literally live on and develop.

In the context of alchemy, Jung also addresses the *Aurora consurgens* in the second lecture on "Dogmas and Natural Symbols." Jung is at this point obviously well acquainted with the text, which he calls "a Pseudo-Thomasian tract of the thirteenth century", expressly dated to Thomas Aquinas' century! (CW II par. 93-94).

This is Jung at his best as a researcher in cultural history, almost as archaeologist and detective in one, tracing and finding unknown sources in the past. However, the purpose, the intention, and the drive in this momentum are his profession as a doctor who diagnoses contemporary diseases, looking for ways to heal and relieve the sufferings of modern man and modern society.

What is "Aurora Consurgens"?

Now, we should not forget the most important thing: what kind of a text are we dealing with? And we have two questions left: When and why this particular text intrigued Jung and prompted him to publish it? When and why? We shall now attempt to answer these questions.

The actual wording of the title: "*Aurora consurgens*" originates in the so-called Vulgate, more specifically, the *Song of Solomon*, chapter 6 verse 9. The *Song of Solomon* is a wonderful hymn about spiritual as well as physical love and longing, and it also celebrates the unification of body and soul. It is a text that explores love as a symbol and reality; carnal longing as integral to the soul's longing, and spirituality as a part of the physical and erotic life; in other words the *coniunctio* as reality, real love, you might say. As a biblical text it has been subject to numerous allegorical interpretations, in Jewish as well as in Christian, and probably also Muslim traditions, and this is still the case even to this day. In the Middle Ages it was a favored text, and many of the well-known medieval theologians have published commentaries on it, including Thomas Aquinas, by the way. However, the title is ambivalent. The reason is that *Aurora*, the goddess of the dawn, dates from the mythology and philosophy of antiquity. *Aurora* is the goddess of the dawn, who wakes up and emerges from the darkness before the sun shows its face. The dawn is both the separation and the unification of night and day, light and darkness. As such, what we could call the *Aurora* thought plays a part in the text entitled *Aurora consurgens*, because the first person narrator describes unification with the deity on the celestial and terrestrial levels, as well as on divine and human levels. The treatise ends with a description of this *coniunctio* in the early dawn – lifted from and inserted among obvious quotes from the *Song of Solomon*. This condition is neither one of total light nor of total darkness; it embodies both. This also means that as an historical text, the *Aurora consurgens* is a blend of two different traditions; on the one hand the Gnostic paradigm of antiquity, the pagan spirituality, and on the other the Christian paradigm. The *Aurora consurgens* shows how these two opposed traditions blend, or are experienced as connected.

The author seeks to express this cognitive experience without consideration for contemporary canonical dogmatic credos, and regardless of any objections others might have. In a sense, the text expresses a reality of the soul and its numinous experience, and the author wishes to share his insights with his contemporaries. Via the Arabian texts on natural sciences and alchemy, the author is evidently acquainted with the pre-Christian modes of thought found in antiquity.

A significant feature of the text is that the euphoric celebration of *Eros* in the final pages is initiated by an encounter with the unexpected. Naturally, Jung's curiosity is aroused by the information that a "suppressed" text exists, as stated in Waldkirch's preface. However, only when he is in possession of the complete text is Jung able to form an impression of what is actually at stake. In 1936, when Emma Jung presumably returned from the Bibliothèque Nationale in Paris, bringing a copy of a manuscript with the full wording, Jung realized what Waldkirch had been shy of printing. The very first lines must have called something up in Jung. The author is obviously a man of the church. He knows the *Vulgate* (the Latin Bible) by heart and is also enthusiastic about the new texts about the philosophers' stone and "the Great Work," then newly translated from Arabic. The Arabian sages such as Senior and Morienus are just as alive and present as the familiar figures of Paul and John, or the disciples of the New Testament. However, the author is evidently obsessed with expressing a new discovery, namely the fact that there is a correspondence between the non-Christian Arabian alchemy and philosophy of science, and the Christian teachings in the biblical texts; between the wondrous stone, "the stone that does not deceive", and Christ, the cornerstone which the builders rejected. The author's tone of voice is at this point also intimate and he seems to be very anxious to tell about an experience, something that has happened.

In *Psychology and Alchemy*, first published in 1944, Jung spends 6-8 pages discussing central themes from the text, and the introduction takes up the major part of his commentaries and parallels. (CW 12 pars. 464-479). The text begins with an introductory presentation of the biblical wisdom, the creative thought of God, from which the world or the cosmos originated, the wise thought that continuously creates the cosmos and unites it, while also constituting the inherent meaning of all things. The concept of the wise thought is also known in the philosophy of antiquity, but here in the *Aurora* text, the focus is on a real life meeting, because the figure is experienced on a personal level. That makes a fundamental difference. From being an abstract thought or an established mythological allegory, it becomes a personal real life experience, a touching attentive presence which affects and thereby changes the narrator, the author of the text. This meeting is, as it were, the text's most important message, the new understanding, or a subject the author feels strongly about. This is a dialogue with his soul. Nobody would have worried if the author had called his book about the new profoundly individual realization or mode of insight – a *Liber Novus* instead of *Aurora consurgens*.

Wisdom in the Earth

So what is different about this specific text? It soon becomes obvious that the biblical female protagonist speaks as a living being not just from the heavenly spheres or from the throne of God on high, but from the depths of the soul. In the first parable, this figure of wisdom says: "Who is the man that liveth, knowing and understanding, delivering my soul from the hand of hell? They that explain me shall have eternal life, and to him I will give to eat of the tree of life which is in paradise, and to sit with me on the throne of my kingdom." (Von Franz, 1966 p. 59). And in the last parable, before the final conjunction with the human being, the woman says in hindsight: "There was darkness over the earth, because I stick fast in the mire of the deep and my reality is not disclosed, out of the depths have I cried ... I called and there was none to answer me." (ibid., pp. 134-135). She is the queen of heaven and the voice of the deep – a divine being, who needs a devoted relation to humanity's knowledge and insight.

Simultaneously recognizable, radically different, and perhaps even influenced by Arabian texts, this archetypal voice of wisdom addresses humanity from the depths of the earth. Her purpose is that the mutual realization, their consensus, expressed in the sentence "how wonderful it is for two people to live as one," should liberate both of them with the momentum of the shared, transformative eros that is otherwise extremely rare in the philosophy of the middle ages and seems so absent in the theology conceived in the name of the Trinity with the Father, Son and Holy Spirit. This is gnosis and insight almost larger than life and expressed in the language of the Bible and the Song of Solomon! Jung must have felt that he had found the hidden treasure. His intention to publish the text most likely stems from that actual moment, when he read the text for the first time.

When was the Concrete Decision made?

When was the concrete decision made? The decision must have been made in the autumn or the winter of 1942, at the latest. In the first edition of *Psychology and Alchemy* published in 1944, the preface is dated January 1943. On page 510 a note indicates that the text, prepared by "M.-L. von Franz, will be soon published in vol. 6 of Psychological Dissertations." However, 13 years were to go by before it was published. This course of events makes it evident that the decision to publish the *Aurora consurgens* was thus made *before* January 1943. Naturally, we cannot identify the *earliest* point in time when this decision was made. Jung mentions the existence of the text in the *Eranos-Jahrbuch* in August 1936, in *Psychology and Religion* from 1938, and briefly in *Paracelsica* from 1941. In none of these publications does he mention that it will be published or that there are plans for a complete publication of the entire text.

It is my estimate that Jung most likely made up his mind to publish the manuscript during the first or the second year of WWII; that is between 1939 and 1942. These are the darkest years, *autumn 1942*, perhaps the darkest hour of the twentieth century; after the fall of France, after Dunkerque, the autumn of 1942 is still long before D-Day.

Perhaps just prior or concurrent with the battle of Stalingrad, the first defeat of Nazism, and the first realistic hope of Allied victory in the future, a light in the darkness.

Why "Aurora"?

Now, we saw the crucial moment in Jung's professional work around 1928-29, in which he received the *Secret of the Golden Flower*. Jung began to discover alchemy and hermetic philosophy – at least in a new significance. We have followed the evolution forward. Now it is time to look back from that particular moment – and conclude this paper.

At this time Jung apparently makes a decision *not* to go ahead with a possible publication of the *Liber Novus, The Red Book*. As previously mentioned: Jung closes *The Red Book* around 1930, but at the same time, he opens the *Artis Auriferae*, the collection of strange texts, that have been waiting on his desk. Here he discovers Conrad Waldkirch's preface, indicating the possible existence of the *Aurora consurgens*. From this point onwards he tries to track it down and, as we now know, five years later he finds it in a roundabout way. Here he encounters a text about wisdom personified, speaking and even shouting from the depths of the earth. However, the book that Jung closes, the *Liber Novus*, is characterized by central experiences and imaginary conversations that were initiated *prior* to WWI. Jung began to make a fair copy of this book in1915 at the height of the insanity of the war. If we return to the beginning of *The Red Book*, we might find some informative perspectives that can help us answer the question *why* – and how the *Aurora consurgens* might be connected as it closes Jung's work?

The ambition to diagnose the contemporary society was evidently inspired by Friedrich Nietzsche's epochal work *Thus Spake Zarathustra*

(1885). In the heyday of the Enlightenment and in the middle of scientific positivism, Nietzsche proclaimed the existence of an overlooked depth perspective in the world, in human existence: *Die Welt ist tief*, "The World Is Deep" as it says in the midnight roundelay in R. J. Hollingdale's translation: "Now I awake at dreaming's end: / The world is deep, / And deeper than the day can comprehend. / Deep is its woe." The last sentence could mean that the reach of the unconscious extends far beyond what diurnal consciousness can comprehend – and encompass, that the unconscious in accordance with its own conceptual logic transcends consciousness, as Jung points out. Already in Jung's first publications there are clear, strong references to Nietzsche's work. From November 1914 Jung reads Zarathustra closely (Shamdasani, 2012 p. 77), and the following year he begins to make a fair copy of *Liber Novus*. After the quotes from Esajas and Paul in the Latin Bible, the first main motif in the book – in fact the opening of the central text in the first chapter – the reader meets a "we." This "we" must be the self-conscious European human being in the years leading up to 1914, who lives in a time that is influenced by two voices or rather: we live in the voice of our time and that voice is all we hear. It is the voice of the times or the dominant contemporary voice, the consciousness that knows and enjoys listening to itself. However, at the same time there is a presentiment of another voice that tries to make itself heard. The first is *die Stimme der Zeit,* and the other is *die Stimme der Tiefe*, the voice of the deep. The identification of the two different voices and their mutual relationship, or lack of relationship, actually their explicit *lack* of consensus is, as mentioned, the opening motif of the strange book.

In this experimental "new book" *Liber Novus,* Jung attempts by way of introduction to listen to the voice of the deep and allow it to speak. Evidently, this entails a certain prophetic mode in the beginning of the book, but the intention is not to become a new prophet or the mouthpiece of a god. As the modern editor Sonu Shamdasani reminds us: "Nietzsche proclaimed that God is dead, whereas the *Liber Novus* describes the rebirth of the divinity in the soul." (Shamdasani 2012 p. 77) Later in the book Jung takes an intimate look at the depths or lets himself be drawn into the deep – probably also inspired by Dante's *Divine Comedy*. In these depths, there are no ecstatic "primal screams" of hitherto unseen hallucinations. What he finds here is a vital evocation of biblical and classical characters and protagonists who, so to speak, walk out of the representations of archaeological findings depicted on pages in learned books. "In these depths, we do not find pure experiences as such, no 'primal scream,' but biblical and classical figures," as Shamdasani points out (ibid., p. 100). Illustrations of named as well as presumed, or as yet unknown characters come to life, find a voice, express independent thoughts and engage in experimental and unpredictable dialogues. The unconscious is not explored as a philosophical or a theological abstraction, but in a manner of speaking as a living re-memorizing and experiencing of the forgotten or overlooked history. It is a conscious as well as a willful attempt at articulating those depths whose dimensions till then only Nietzsche had explored. The past is a living presence.

Back to the Middle Ages – within Ourselves

It is in this perspective that we should attempt to understand something of what Jung attempts to capture experimentally in *his* "medieval" book. As he himself states in it: "I must catch up with a piece of the Middle Ages – within myself. We have only finished the Middle Ages – of others." (RB p. 330; Shamdasani, 2012 p. 130).

Here is an "I" – and a "we." *The Red Book* is, by the way, *also* a literary work, and Jung, or the first person narrator –– attempts consciously to extract and fixate something that has been lost in the Middle Ages. Most likely his impulse was based on the presumption that the Middle Ages were characterized by a philosophy and a psychology in which the soul was perceived as a substance, something real with an objective existence as opposed to the voice of the modern times that had developed a "psychology without soul." Modern humanity has only removed itself from the Middle Ages in time, and not developed accordingly. Hence from 1915 Jung writes and illuminates the *Liber Novus* as a medieval manuscript, a genuine *codex*. He imitates the abbreviations and out of concern for the reader, he even provides an overview of the abbreviation system prior to the text. He even decapitalizes the nouns, as was the practice in medieval German prior to the mid sixteenth century. In an attempt to negotiate a certain "knowledge" or science of the soul, of the history of past culture and psychology, something we have forgotten or just removed ourselves from. That is one major task of the experiment: to write and experience the lost aspects of culture. Just like the contemporary marine archaeologists in Roskilde who with their own hands rebuilt Viking ships down to the minutest detail, because the manual craftsmanship brought an insight in, and the experience of the methods and approaches of the past, which the deskwork and computer animations of today are unable to replicate. In the same way and for the same reason Jung wanted to *write* a Medieval book with his own hands, to craft it physically in order to extract and approach the mentality of the past, to seek and find the forgotten knowledge of the soul, the ignored voice of the deep and to allow the voice of the unconscious, of nature, to speak again in a truly *liber novus*. The "new book" is an "old" Medieval book with a new textual content that recovers what has been lost and locates it in a contemporary context – this was true for Jung's ambition with "The Red Book" and this was true for the author of _Aurora consurgens_ – to give a voice to the past in the present. This actually brings "The Red Book" in connection with the medieval mind, especially the 12th Century, more than the scholastic 13th century that is the century of Hildegard of Bingen, Bernardus Silvestris and Ioachim of Fiore with their imaginative way of thinking. The historian becomes a kind of therapist – "the therapy of our time" as James Hillman puts it in a published conversation with Sonu Shamdasani (Hillman, 2013, p. 98).

Conclusion

Jung closed the _Liber Novus_ because, as he writes in 1959, the discovery of alchemy was actualized, that is, the content found a way to be worked out into a scientific work. The actualization occurred by way of the discovery of the alchemical and the hermetic traditions in European history and the significance that Jung gives to this "rejected knowledge." (Hanegraaff, 2012). However, it also became a quest for and a real discovery of a forgotten Medieval book – in reality. Jung seemingly rejected the thought of publishing _The Red Book_ at least in his own lifetime, and would not regard it as a work of art either. There was too much responsibility connected to the contents. Instead of publishing the book that would complete the Middle Ages as a kind of an artistic skill, Jung had the opportunity as a scientist to publish the discovery from the Middle Ages that he felt an imperative to return to, in order to develop modern culture. It was at once an individual and a collective experience, a task for an "I" and a "we." Jung wanted to express and amplify his personal experience in the scientific language of his time – and that impulse is the context of his many, deep and challenging interpretations of the texts on alchemy and Hermetic philosophy. A similar ambition is the driving force of the author of _Aurora_ – whoever he is. He wishes to express a deep religious, that is emotional and cognitive, experience of the knowledge of the past, but also a desire to mediate it to his contemporaries in the language of his own day and age. This language is characterized by the biblical quotes and the new scientific literatures that had recently been translated from Arabic and were received with enthusiasm by most.

Jung discovered with the _Aurora consurgens_ a light in the darkness – and he allowed it to shine, and decided that it should be published at the very darkest moment of the century. In so doing, Jung (and von Franz) did not necessarily prepare intercultural dialogues across the globe, like the _golden flower_ that had initiated it all, but a golden hour for the dialogue all cultures face as a challenge, a task: a dialogue between the knowledge of the past and the knowledge of the present. We are constantly in danger of losing the spirit of the depths – a voice from nature, from the unconscious. In my view, that is a major challenge to humanity in the twenty-first century. Jung's studies in alchemy and Jung's and von Franz's publication of the *Aurora consurgens* is in that respect a help and an inspiration to us all, which we have not yet recognized.

Bibliography

Hanegraaff, W. J. (2012) *Esotericism and the Academy. Rejected Knowledge in Western Culture*, Cambridge: Cambridge University Press.

Hillman, J. & Shamdasani, S. (2013) *The Lament of the Dead*, New York: W.W. Norton.

Härtel, H, Ekowski, F.(1982) *Handschriften der Niedersächsischen Landesbibliothek*, Hannover, 2. Teil, Wiesbaden

Jung, C. G. (1952) [1944], *Psychology and Alchemy, Collected Works* Vol. 12, London: Routledge and Kegan Paul.

Jung, C. G (1967) [1929], *Commentary on "The Secret of the Golden Flower", Alchemical Studies, Collected Works* Vol. 13.London: Routledge and Kegan Paul.

Jung, C. G. (1977) *Psychology and Religion. East and West Collected Works* Vol. 11, London: Routledge and Kegan Paul.

Jung, C. G. (1977a) *The Symbolic Life, Collected Works* Vol. 18, London: Routledge and Kegan Paul.

Jung, C. G. (2009) *The Red Book (Liber Novus)* ed. Sonu Shamdasani, New York: W.W. Norton & Company.

Johannes Rhenanus (1625) ed. *Harmoniae inperscrutabilis chymico-philosophicae sive Philosophorum antiquorum consententium decades duae*, Frankfurt

Shamdasani, S. (2012) *C.G. Jung: A Biography in Books*, New York: W.W. Norton & Company.

von Franz, Marie-Louise (1966) *Aurora consurgens. A Dokument Attributed to Thomas Aquinas on the Problem of Opposites in Alchemy.* A Companion Work to C.G. Jung's *Mysterium Coniunctionis*, Translated by R.F.C. Hull and A.S.B. Glover, London: Routledge and Kegan Paul.

The Analytic Process as a Play of Changing Perspectives in the Analyst

Gustav Bovensiepen
(Germany, DGAP)

Introduction

Change of Gaze on Different "Cultures"

Today, in trying to reflect on the analytic process as a play with changing perspectives, I primarily focus on the simultaneity of very different forms and ways of psychic proceedings that manifest in the actual analytic situation. I think it is this highly complex simultaneity that constitutes the matrix that forms the analytic couple. That means that a modern analytical treatment technique, in a world where the permeability of different "cultures" (in a comprehensive sense) is changing at high speed, requires that we as analysts have to be particularly flexible in the choice of our perspectives as introspective observers in the analytic situation. A flexible shift, a switch, or be it a reversal of the observer's perspective, a change of gaze on the various internal and external "cultures" that meet in the analytic couple, I regard as crucial. The term "change of gaze" is used here by analogy with a method of modern art history, i.e. the history and theory of gaze (Belting 2008) that led to surprising insights when applied to the art of different cultures.

Consciousness of Play as a Perspective

The "play" of perspectives I understand as a kind of "consciousness of playing" which as an analytic attitude is an essential part of my symbolic stance and of great importance in my work as an analyst. Since Johan Huizinga's "Homo ludens" (1956) we know that playing may be a creative process stimulating the self-organisation of culture. I believe that consciousness of play in the analytic couple facilitates the emergence of psychic meaning. With the non-analytic term for perspective I want to emphasize the space and sphere character of the analytic couple's matrix. The "analytical object", or what happens in analysis, can be observed and explored from very different perspectives. The transference/countertransference perspective is very central but it is not the only one. "Perspicere", looking through the abundance of the "material" emerging in the session towards an imaginal horizon may admit us access to the unconscious of the analytic couple. In such a case, things that we can explore and think about may then become visible.

Unfolding Transcendent Function in "Vigorous Moments of Being"

I see the essence of my analytical work primarily in those moments where the unspeakable suddenly becomes namable, hearable, visible, tangible or perceptible with our senses, i.e. when the non-thinkable (cf. Alvarez 1998) or the not-yet-accessible or unthinkable becomes accessible. In Ogden's words (2004) it is a need occurring in the analytic situation as a "moment of vivid desire, of impulse or need to express the not-yet-articulated" (p. 15). Or, as can be said about some analytic situations, when something dead comes to life. In her autobiographical "sketch of the past" Virginia Woolf (2002) speaks of the "vigorous moments of being". These are "sporadic moments of sudden experience of perception and presence" (K. Reichert, 2012, p. XV), which are embedded in yet much more numerous moments of "non-being in a kind of indefinite cotton wool" (Woolf 2002, p. 83/84) as she described the everyday struggling along, the routine, her social obligations and her work.

When the analytic couple succeeds in expressing the non-thinkable, in experiencing a "vigorous moment of being", this in my view complies with the immediate experience of the transcendent function; the transcendent function is actually happening in such moments.

In terms of the alchemistic imagery for the analytic process, I shall operate with a kind of lunar awareness in my reflections (cf. Jung, CW 14/I, §§ 149 ff.) – an attitude that attempts to connect reverie and intuition with the bringing ideas to life.

Places of Being in the Dream – Area of Retreat or Transition

Analyst's Dream in the Presence of Peter: "Are you sleeping?"

First of all I want to describe to you a little vignette of the work with an eight-year-old boy I will call Peter. It is a scene from a quite advanced treatment phase.

Peter was an intelligent boy who grew up in an emotionally sparse environment. He came to see me because of great contact problems. In one session I observed Peter carefully pushing little human figures that he had formed out of playdough into a house made of wooden building blocks. He was deeply lost in his play, patiently and carefully trying to fiddle the little figures into the house. I was in a somewhat tired, but relaxed condition, feeling an easy and thoughtless void watching him. Peter was faintly mumbling to himself. I did not understand what he was saying, with his voice getting softer and softer as I began to doze off. Then I heard myself speaking in a dream; I was annoyed, almost angry. I heard myself say, "This is my room, you're kindly supposed to ask me when you want to pass through!" I was in my room in the house where I grew up in childhood. I was very annoyed with one of my sisters who indeed had to pass through my room to reach her own. This had occasionally caused heavy quarrelling about the "right of way". Then I heard a curious and friendly voice in the dream asking, "Are you sleeping?" I became wide awake again. Peter looked up from his play and repeated his question kindly and placidly, "Are you sleeping?" I felt somewhat embarrassed and said appeasingly: "Yes, I guess I dozed off a bit and was just thinking to myself." Peter drily answered, "It's OK, you just think to yourself and I'll carry on here."

The Accessibility of Psychic Space

What might have happened? Peter was an only child and was often teased and excluded by the other children as a little all-knowing "professor". He withdrew to his home and had no friends. So it is easy to assume that he enacted a familiar situation in this scene, i.e. the fearful withdrawal from the other children into his safe home, but at the price of isolation. So he had no problem in allowing himself and me, too, a separate room of withdrawal. Yet the relaxed and patient condition he showed in his playing did not fit in. His fear of the other children, their aggressiveness and his own aggressive affects were missing in the scene, other than the scene in my dream: I was angry in the dream and struggling for my sovereign right on the transit through my room. I defended it against my sister's intrusion, but could not quite prevent it, as I had to live in the transit room. This scene contained an experience well known to me: growing up with many brothers and sisters I often had to fight for my own space. But that was not Peter's problem. From the perspective of transference/countertransference one might assume that Peter had split off his defended affects of fear and rage and moved them into me thus triggering my childhood scene. Yet, this view does not convince me clinically, so I take a change in perspective: perhaps my internal re-enactment of my childhood situation was triggered uniquely by the little figures' direction of movement into the house. Peter in contrast presumably enacted his desire of accessibility to his internal mother/the therapist. Peter was a child who had scarcely experienced finding a place in his mother's psyche; she was, psychologically, out of reach for him. The therapist was not out of reach, but in a condition of "thoughtless void" and responsive. For Peter, the play scene did not have the violent aspect that sometimes appertained to the transit fights of my childhood.

His house made of building blocks acquired the function of the third for the analytic couple. Playing in my presence made him discover a psychic space where he and I could fantasize. During this session he began to think about how he could manage to invite his classmates to his home – although this idea, and how they would stay in his room, caused him a lot of fear. So he started to deal with thoughts/fantasies that previously had been unthinkable for him.

When initially speaking of the not-yet-thinkable thoughts or fantasies, I wanted to express that it may also be about things in the future. I understand Jung's prospective-final tendency of the unconscious as the area where these not-yet-thinkable thoughts or fantasies are stored and we as therapists can hope to function as obstetricians to bring them to life and make them accessible.

In the above paragraph, *the accessibility of the psychic space* engaged me in what in itself enables many perspectives – according to where the ego and parts of the self "live", inside or outside, locked in or locked out, included or excluded, whether the room is a shelter or a prison, a room full of life and treasures or a room hostile to life, a claustrum etc. The struggle for the accessibility of the internal space often dominates the analytic process for a long time.

Psychic Space Without Horizon: Vanishing of the Space by the Abundance of Thoughts

Spatialization of Thoughts: Bion

In his "Poetics of Space" the French philosopher Gaston Bachelard (1987, p. 211) speaks of the "spatialization of thoughts" – this, too, is a form of visualization of the unthinkable. Don't we permanently deal in our dreams, in our consulting rooms and in our thinking spaces with "stray" and roving thoughts and fantasies? As therapists we try to be responsive to those "thoughts", but we do not always succeed.

In the Italian seminars, Bion recommended to the participants, in an almost playful and easy way, a receptive attitude towards their patients for the next day:

I suggest this view where you are vulnerable to anything that your senses will tell you: as you watch, you begin to narrow it down, and then ask yourself why you are acting in that way. That depends on daring to feel or think whatever you feel or think. I have spoken of it before as a situation in which all sorts of thoughts are flying around—the patient gets rid of all his thoughts which then, in my pictorial imagination, are flying around. If you can be wide open, then I think there is a chance that you might catch some of those wild thoughts. And if you allow them to lodge in your mind, however ridiculous, however stupid, however fantastic, then there may be a chance of having a look at them. That is a matter of daring to have such thoughts—never mind whether you are supposed to have them or not—and keeping them long enough to be able to formulate what they are (Bion 2005, The Italian Seminars, Rome, 13 July 1977).

The Attitude of Lessened Attention

In the consulting room we are often surrounded by a host of feelings, fantasies, impulses, and actions of our patients as well as our own thoughts, often in confusing abundance. It is difficult then to find a kind of order or sense and to keep up our thinking ability. The attempt to create meaningful connections will often fail. I rather concentrate on taking a conscious attitude of lessened attention and try not to actively hold or understand anything. I remain very passive instead, as if the patient's talking were just background music. I may feel an affect then, have a picture, notice a physical sensation or it can be just a word that gets caught or a thought becoming verbalized or an idea that I start thinking about. The most crucial seems to be that beyond our theoretical beliefs we are also open to our own thoughts and perspectives that permanently accompany us in the treatment, and may connect with our analysands' thoughts buzzing around in the therapeutic room.

Child analyst Anne Alvarez writes on the psychic power of "thoughts":

> A mind is a vast panorama of thought-about feelings and felt-about thoughts that are constantly in interaction with one another. They are dynamic and energetic. Thoughts have their own power of existence.
>
> (Alvarez 1998, p. 218 f.)

And I would say in addition that this power requires taming a defined psychic space, yet a space with a horizon.

Psychic Space With Horizon

How Ideas become Graspable: Infant Observation

Even the first – intrauterine – sensory experiences are acoustic and spatial: the spatial experience is presumably pioneered by the experience of motion and noises. The infant's spatial experience in the relationship with the first objects depends on the mother's way of holding the baby as well as on the baby's gaze perspective on the mother and the mother's gaze perspective on the baby. Alvarez contributes to this:

> [T]here are "notions such as the object's availability, its accessibility, graspability, proximity and its perceptual followability. … The conditions under which babies are able to reach and grasp objects in three-dimensional space may also be of relevance to the question of the conditions under which an *idea* may begin to become graspable" (Alvarez 1992, p. 77 f.).

To illustrate the effect of a change of perspective and gaze between mother and child and the structuring of psychic space by motion, I want to describe a short episode from a psychoanalytic infant observation[1].

When the observation took place, baby Paul was six weeks old. By then, Paul and his mother had not yet found a sufficiently attuned rhythm together. They also had difficulties in breastfeeding. During the observation the first satisfying breastfeeding situation took place. The observer writes:

> When Paul seems to have finished and went on sucking a bit on his mother's nipple in a dreamy and playful way with his eyes closed, mother pulls her breast away saying strictly: "Not like that!" She takes him up for a burp tapping him on the back fast and regularly. When no burp would come she puts him to her breast again. Paul shortly sucks again, but does not seem to be hungry anymore. He lies there without moving and glances into the distance. He repeatedly sticks out his tongue. He seems to make sucking movements. Mother bends down into Paul's visual field and also sticks out her tongue. She looks like she wants to mirror his actions, but appears rather clumsy and tense. Then she takes Paul up again and he finally burps. Now she holds him calmly in her arm. It is the first time that I experience the situation as relaxed and placid. Just as I want to leave with a good feeling in my stomach, Paul looks at his mother with a broad smile. I am surprised and at the same time happy and touched. The mother, too, seems to be quite surprised. This is the second time that he is smiling, she says happy and moved. I am also moved by this beautiful picture with the two of them and happily say good-bye. As I get dressed in the hallway and get ready to leave the apartment, the mother comes out once more with Paul in her arm and says "Thank you". I am a bit confused, but then I feel a mixture of relief and happiness.

---

1   I want to thank my colleague, Ms Julia Hillen, for allowing me to quote from her infant observation report.

The Imaginal Gaze

During this observation scene a vivid exchange of glances happened for the first time between Paul and his mother. Both the mother-child couple and the observer experienced it with deep emotion and a happy feeling. The mother's gratefulness may unconsciously have been directed to the observer because she *in the mother's place* had taken the function of the container for Paul and could observe him with a "thinking", "imaginal" gaze. His mother had not understood his first attempts – playing with the nipple when his hunger was satisfied – to establish and explore a psychic space between himself and his mother. Only when he repeatedly stuck out his tongue she could receive and imitate it. The observer and the seminar group first thought it was a continued sucking (on the imagined breast); and perhaps that was also true. Yet today I understand it as a rudimentary form of a gesture by which Paul emphasized his gaze and gave a perspective to the "indefinite" space between himself and his mother by a movement towards her. Thus the "indefinite" space became "definite" with the mother's attentive facial expression as a defining horizon. Vladimir Nabokov starts his autobiography with the phrase: „The cradle swings above an abyss".[1] Only when the mother holds the child in the "right" distance the indefinite space becomes definite, where imagination can take place. Thus anxiety can be reduced.

Virginia Woolf (2002) describes how threatening the child's perspective can be in apparently unlimited space:

> It seems to me that a child must have a curious focus; it sees an air-ball or a shell with extreme distinctness; I still see the air-balls, blue and purple, and the ribs on the shells; but these points are enclosed in vast empty spaces. How large for instance was the space beneath the nursery table! I see it still as a great black space with the table-cloth hanging down in folds on the outskirts in the distance … The night nursery was vast too. In winter I would slip in before bed to take a look at the fire. I was very anxious to see that the fire was low, because it frightened me if it burnt after we went to bed. I dreaded that little flickering flame on the walls and I looked and looked and could not sleep; and in order to have company, said "What did you say, Nessa?" although she was asleep, to wake her and to hear someone's voice (p. 90/91).

The child's imagination lights up by the „little flickering flame on the walls". And it evokes fear when the child feels alone with them in a huge room that she experiences without horizon, without a human companion.

---

1   My thanks to Angelica Löwe for drawing my attention to this remarkable sentence.

The Analytic State of Consciousness as a Mentality of Play and Reversal of Perspective

Play State of the Patient's Consciousness

Winnicott phrased the understanding of the analytic couple's consciousness as a consciousness of play in his famous statement:

"Psychotherapy takes place in the overlap of two areas of playing, that of the patient and that of the therapist. Psychotherapy has to do with two people playing together." (Winnicott 1971 p. 37) The American analyst Frankel (2011) says (about the analysis with adults), that according to the degree of the patient's regression and their increasing confidence, we can refer to a play state of the patient's consciousness, which can help the patient to amplify particular facts of their experience (p. 1421).

Without getting into details now, we can say that there is a great structural similarity between the consciousness of play and the consciousness of dream – the way unconscious thinking is organized.

If we take the intersubjective character of the analytic situation seriously there are, by analogy to the mother-infant dialogue, reversed conditions of interpretation and meaning: I, the therapist, am the baby then who does not yet understand the patients' "language", the meaning of their statements, but has to learn them arduously. So, it is very seductive to use our "knowledge" instead, even that of the archetypical images and symbols, in order to denominate what may not be accessible, hard to bear or confusing, not yet thinkable. This may lead to premature interpretations or to the analysand's adaptation to the analyst's language. An analytic attitude as consciousness of play could be protective against this dominance of knowledge.

A question, also resulting from the analytic couple's mentality of play, is that of the therapist's appropriate responsiveness: How active or even expressive are we as therapists entitled to be, or how strongly withdrawn do we have to be in terms of the evenly suspended attention in order to still maintain a responsive emotional presence? A mentality of play also opens up more symmetry in the activity of the two participants of the analytic couple. I do not want to deny the structural asymmetry of the analytic situation. As a child therapist I am familiar with the necessity of more activity or even initiative from the therapist's side, yet in a different way this also applies to the analytic work with adults.

The (Jungian) Analyst as a "Lively Object"

As therapists, we need a certain degree of joy of playing with objects, thoughts, fantasies. It is here that I primarily locate the meaning of amplification and active imagination and other Jungian methods: It is not the content of the "material" that is important in the first place, but the fact that liveliness is maintained in us as analysts, that our patients can experience us as a "thinking", i.e. graspable "lively object" (Alvarez 2001), an experience that many of them could not have in their childhood. This playful perspective or attitude is also maintained by the Israeli psychoanalyst, Bitan (2012) who sees the playfulness of the psychoanalytic situation therein – that the "psyches" of therapist and patient can exist side by side in a kind of peaceful coexistence. Bitan writes:

> I suggest that the intersubjective matrix is founded on playful relations between oppositions that are no longer grasped as con-tradictory, but rather as interwoven. The therapeutic situation is explored as an attempt to create a playful space in which the patient and therapist are not two distinct and exclusive entities but rather "peacefully coexist" (Bitan 2012, p. 30).

I am very fond of this attitude of playful relationship coexistence as it facilitates the change of gaze when our Jungian thinking is too caught up in the psychology of opposites. The playful symmetry of perspectives becomes the more obvious the more we focus on the unconscious stream of thoughts, the unconscious thinking.

The Organization of Unconscious Thinking

Peter's Blocks are Evocative Objects

To me unconscious thinking is like the flowing of a river that alters the shores and edges of our consciousness so that it brings forth the characteristic permanent shiftings of the shore, the topography, the "landscape of complexes" (Kast 1990) by the power of the water. The unconscious thinking as an interpretation of our world permanently goes on in us, and the possibilities of design, of forms, are potentially infinite. This is what Bollas means by saying that anyone of us secretly is a novelist, composer, painter, dancer. By means of language, sound, picture and motion we compose thousands of unconscious thoughts about the world we live in (cf. Bollas 2009).

Any object in our outside world can become an "evocative object", which means that any ordinary object can potentially trigger memo-ries and unconscious processes. The building blocks in my consulting room (cf. Peter's play) are particularly suitable by their geometrically clear and abstract – "empty" – form to evoke, receive and develop the unconscious thoughts that are projected into the outside world.

Based on the scientific evaluation of tape-recorded reports of psychoanalytic treatments (cf. ESGUT/IPA) it can be shown how the therapist's receptive unconscious takes in the patient's unconscious and organizes this material as unconscious thinking.

The Many "Logics" of Unconscious Thinking

Freud had assumed a serial logic, a logic of sequence of the unconscious thinking which can give the incoherent and volatile verbal associations meaning and shape.

I believe that the unconscious thinking does not exclusively follow a serial logic. There are probably many different organizational principles of the unconscious of which we know just a very small part. For example, the unconscious thinking in pictures, which is so important to us Jungians, does not primarily follow a serial logic but rather a spatial logic and a logic of gaze of which I will say more later. The compensatory relationship of the unconscious to consciousness is not of serial logic either, nor is it the final-prospective aspect of the unconscious.

When we turn to the therapist's unconscious I am sure that the patient's projections in our psyche are not only organized in the way it happens in the patient, but also in the way *our own thoughts and fantasies* are unconsciously organized in our own psyche. My dream of the struggle about the transit room in the session with Peter might be an example of this. Bion's container metaphor of the psyche is clinically plausible and useful, but it overstresses the receptive and passive character of the analyst's psyche. It is rather an analytic attitude, but not an organizational model of unconscious thinking. The same applies to the "contagion" metaphor in Jung's "Psychology of Transference" (Jung CW 16). Beyond the cycle of projection or projective identification and introjection as modi of unconscious communication, we react as therapists – within the field of transference and countertransference – independently, with our own way of thinking and organizing unconscious contents. This would be a further perspective in order to creatively alter the intersubjective ensemble, the psychic space of the analytic couple.

The Imaginal Place as The Third: The Gaze out of the Window

An Art History of Gaze: the Visualization of Mental Images

In a fascinating work, the art historian and cultural scientist, Hans Belting (2008), develops a western-eastern history of gaze based on the example of the discovery of perspective in the art of the renaissance. He shows that "the art of perspective [in the renaissance] was based on a theory of Arabian origin, the mathematic theory of the lines of sight and the geometry of light" (p. 9) of the Arabian mathematician Alhazen who lived in the 11th century, and whose writings on optics and philosophy were known and valued up to the high Middle Ages. Belting emphasizes that "in the Arabian theory of sight a monopoly was granted to the imageless light whereas the images were relegated solely to the mental area" (p. 11), which means they were visualized images that were – for various reasons – not displayed. This Arabian theory of sight was expressed in the geometric forms strictly based on mathematics e.g. of the muquarnas (**Picture 1 and 2**) and in the window grilles of the maschrabiyya (**Picture 3, 4**). The potential space for mental images in this culturally determined, abstract, mathematically-geometrically established imaginal practice seems to be almost indefinitely vast.

The alteration of the imaginal practice, the "quantum leap [of the renaissance] was now that it brought the gaze and with it the gazing subject into the picture. It is art-historically fascinating that an Arabian theory of gaze with its geometric abstraction was reconceived in western thinking against its original sense into an imaginal theory that makes the human gaze pivotal in any perception and captures it in pictures" (Belting 2008/2011 p. 12). The gaze gives the subject a position in space, and the perspective from which we view a picture determines our relation to the picture and vice versa: a picture looks at us or it does not (**Picture 5 and 6**). I recall the baby Paul I referred to earlier, and the importance of the perspective from which the infant views his mother and is positioned before her. With the invention of the perspective in art, the gaze out of the window, the so called windows view, and the significance of the horizon, become highly important for the western art of painting and remain popular until the beginning of the 19th century. The window metaphor in the art of painting opened the subject's gaze to the outside, into a world that actually offers and imaginatively displays an inside view. The metaphor of the window that opens a view into the human soul originates from this time when the perspective was discovered.

Now I will report a vignette where we also deal with the windows view which led to the emergence of the "third" in the analytic situation and thus to the animation of my own psychic space.

1. Alhambra, Granada: The cupola of the hall of the two sisters, around about 1230 (Belting 2008, p. 133)

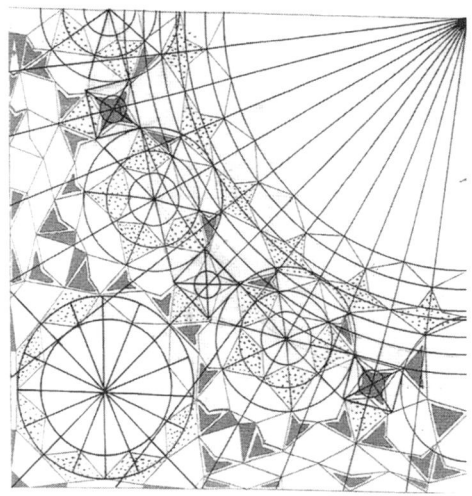

2: *Architectural drawing, Iran around about 1500, Topkapi Museum, Istanbul*

3: Maschrabiyya at a palace in Kairo (wikipedia.org/wiki/Maschrabiyya)

4. Hassan Fathy, room in New-Gourna, around Luxor 1950 (Belting 2008, p .275)

5. Lorenz Stoer, draft of "Geometrie et Perspectiva", 1567 (Graphic Collection Munich)

6. Bernadino Licinio (?), picture of an architect (?) and self-portrait of the painter, 1520/30 (Museum Würzburg)

7. View from my consulting room in Winter

8. View form my consulting room in Spring

9. View from my consulting room in Summer

Living in a Closed Internal World (Claustrum)

Mr. W., a professionally successful engineer in his early fifties, primarily suffered from getting into psychic withdrawals because of conflicts or into states of total isolation where he could not think nor feel nor speak. Mr. W. was deeply convinced that he could not really give love. When he thought he was criticized, he felt "annihilated" as he put it. Unconsciously he seemed to be afraid I might find out how devious, phony and destructive he actually was, that somebody might indeed enter his space of withdrawal. On the one hand, he experienced this space like a prison from where he could not escape; on the other hand, he felt safe in it. At the beginning of the analysis he once told me that the most comforting and most safe situation for him was driving his car with windows closed, abundantly farting and feeling incredibly easy in his own stink. This easy feeling even increased when he watched the other drivers in their cars who were not so well off and had no idea of how comfortable he was in his car. In a post-Kleinian view one could easily recognize this phantasy as a variation of the "life in the claustrum" (Meltzer 1992), the unconscious identification of a part of the personality with the anal space of the internal mother. In terms of Erich Neumann's (1974) female archetypes of the unconscious, this patient lived captured in the identification with a hostile-to-life aspect of the Great Mother's negative fundamental character.

For a long time Mr. W. used the analysis to complain about conflicts with his wife and especially to report on his professional activity. Very seldom I felt like getting direct insight into his internal world and his feelings. Sometimes he suddenly briefly communicated aggressive-sadistic or sexual phantasy fragments which I could not understand from the context of the session and which we could not talk about then. I experienced these phantasy fragments as violent blasting pieces from another world. We both unconsciously tended to "defuse" them immediately and consequently could not find access to them. The patient could not fantasize nor report any dreams. He would often lay there in long-lasting silence and seemed to be out of reach; when I addressed this, he said that in his mind he was busy thinking about a technical problem he had at work. I realized that I then got distracted in my own world or I drifted into a mood of resignation. Then I focus my gaze on the beautiful big tree in front of my window (**Picture 9**). I enjoy the high-contrast structure of the branches, the play of light in the leaves at various times of day, the structures and colours changing over the seasons, or the hustle and bustle of the squirrel family that lives in the tree.

The Tree in Front of my Window as the Imaginal Third (Mundus Imaginalis)

In the third year of treatment it occasionally happened that while Mr. W. was silently lying on the couch, and I was trying to get in contact with him, he would talk about being occupied with perceiving (it was winter time) the geometric figures in the branches of the tree, in particular he often saw isosceles triangles (**Picture 7**). I said that maybe he was geometricizing his thoughts and phantasies in order to make them more graspable, but at the same time I explained that I understood this as a resistance, as a flight from the analytic space, as a flight from his phantasies and feelings so as to avoid speaking about them. And I thought without saying it, that now he even started measuring this huge tree in thought. He acknowledged my term "geometricizing of thoughts" approvingly, but without comment.

Subsequently, Mr. W. spoke about the tree again and again describing how it began to change in spring time – it was like speaking about an old friend. When in early summer (**Picture 8 and 9**) the leaves had fully developed he noticed with regret that the branches were no longer visible, so he could not "geometricize" his phantasies any more. In between these comments about the tree Mr. W. repeatedly dozed off. He began dreaming in this condition and had "a lot of phantasies" which unfortunately he could not verbalize, yet they began to arouse great interest in him. So, based on the dreamy condition in the analysis he was now able to look beyond his internal anal prison, to gaze as it were through the grilled window, the maschrabiyya, and discover the hidden, still incomprehensible, yet lively world within himself. Just as parts of him were locked in in the anal claustrum, he felt at the same time being locked out of his lively world. Both his gaze and mine had an almost identical point of view (I would sit close behind the couch), but they met with different psychic perspectives in the branches of the tree: the claustrum projected into the tree in the form of Mr. W.'s geometricized phantasies and my efforts to stay psychically alive, met in the tree. So the tree became the place of intersubjective encounter in terms of the mundus imaginalis (Corbin 1964/1972). It became the imaginal place in the function of the third in the sense that a change of gaze or a reversal of perspective became possible. When I am locked in I am at the same time locked out. To enable again and again a change of gaze, to get a change of perspective, is part of our analytic work.

Just like the stunningly beautiful muquarnas (**Picture 1** Alhambra) and the window grilles of the maschrabiyya (**Picture 4**) the pure form, the structure of the branches of the tree with and without leaves have a great imaginative power. In the same way the simple abstract building blocks always had a great imaginative power as evocative objects both for me and for many of my little patients. I think that the "empty" forms or the play of light and shadow activate the infant's earliest visual perceptive experiences and beside other modalities like voice and motion, presumably play a central part in the first pre-conceptions of thinking and phantasizing.

Conclusion

If we take seriously the idea of the intersubjective matrix as a complex psychic space, then the analytic work requires from us to be ready to change our gaze, to be ready to flexibly play with different perspectives. I have tried to show various perspectives beyond the well-known ones such as conscious/unconscious, transference/countertransference or collective unconscious/personal unconscious, and primarily focused on the concept of psychic space: its accessibility/inaccessibility, its finiteness/infinity, the reversal of perspective as an expression of the psychic couple's mentality of play, the non-linear organization of unconscious thinking and, finally, the gaze out of the consulting room as an imaginal place in the function of the third for the analytic couple. I believe that when we are more frequently capable of a surprising change of gaze or perspective, the evolvement of the transcendent function will be facilitated.

Bibliography

Alvarez, A. (1998): *Failures to Link: Attacks or Defects? Some questions concerning the thinkability of Oedipal and pre-Oedipal thoughts.* J. Child Psychothp. *24 (2): 213 – 231*

Alvarez, A. (1992): *Live Company.* London: Routledge

Bachelard, G. (1987): *Poetik des Raumes.* Frankfurt a.M.: Fischer Taschenbuch Verlag

Belting, H. (2008): *Florenz und Bagdad. Eine westöstliche Geschichte des Blicks* München: C.H. Beck (Florence and Baghdad. Renaissance Art and Arab Science. Translated by Deborah Lucas Schneider, Harvard University Press)

Bion, W.R. (2005): *The Italian Seminars*, London: Karnac

Bitan, S. (2012): „*Winnicott and Derrida: Development of logic of play"*. Int. J Psychoanal 93:29-51

Bollas, Ch. (2009): *The Infinite Question. Routledge*, London: Routlegde

Corbin, H. (1964/1972): Mundus Imaginalis or the Imaginary and the Imaginal. New York, Spring Journal, S. 1-19

ESGUT: European Study Group for Unconscious Thinking (IPV/IPA)

Frankel, J. (2011): The analytic state of consciousness as a form of play and a foundational transference. *The International Journal of Psychoanalysis* 92: 1411-1436

Huizinga, J. (1956): *Homo ludens*. Vom Ursprung der Kultur im Spiel., Reinbek b. Hamburg: Rowohlt

Jung, C.G. (1946) „Psychologie der Übertragung", GW 16 (please complete the reference)

Jung, C.G. (1955/56): Mysterium Coniunctionis. GW 14/1 (please complete the reference)

Kast, V. (1990). *Die Dynamik der Symbole. Grundlagen der Jungschen Psychotherapie*. Olten u. Freiburg: Walter

Meltzer, D. (1992): *The Claustrum. An Investigation of Claustrophic Phenomena*. The Clunie Press

Neumann, E. (1974): Die Große Mutter. Olten und Freiburg: Walter-Verlag

Ogden, Th. H. (2004): *Gespräche im Zwischenreich des Träumens*. Giessen: Psychosozial Verlag (Conversations at the Frontier of Dreaming. Jason Aronson Inc. 2001)

Reichert, K. (2012): „Vorbemerkung" zu V. Woolf, *Augenblicke des Daseins. Autobiographische Skizzen*. Deutsch von B. Walitzek, Frankfurt a.M.: S Fischer

Winnicott, D.W. (1971): *Playing and Reality*. London: Tavistock Publications Ltd.

Woolf V. (2002): *Moments of Being: Autobiographical Writings of Virginia Woolf*. Edited by J. Schulkind. London: Pimlico edition 2002 (Random House)

Tuesday, 20 August 2013

Introduction

Robert Wimmer

Master of Ceremonies

(Germany, DGAP)

Good Morning Dear Colleagues,

As your Master of Ceremonies for today, I hope you had a pleasant night, which prepared you for another day of surprises, new perspectives upon old themes, new themes seen through familiar and unfamiliar spectacles.

The morning, so it seems, is dedicated to Jung and to the adventures of exploring and understanding, not only in the sense of exploring and understanding Jung or his writings but, furthermore, as an attempt to shed some light on the difficult and fragile processes emerging from the encounters with the "loaded' – with meaningful materials as Jung's writings are. This is the first part of this morning's program. It will be followed by fairy tales, in the second part.

While sometimes representatives of other disciplines criticise Jungian concepts of science, theory formation and ways of interaction with patients as "not objective", Jungian traditions implied from the beginning a deep sense of the interwovenness of the "subject" with the "object". The ethologists had no problem finding out that the rat in the maze acts differently if being watched while crossing it. In the 20th century the physicists learned that even the atomic corpuscles seem to "know" that they are being observed. So, the object turned out to be an "object with subjectivity". Few researchers and theorists dared to go ahead and ask the question how the researcher, the supposedly only subject in the procedure, becomes the object of his "object" and of the process of the observation itself. What Hegel and others postulated in the concepts of dialectics is in the very essence of the Jungian view on the world, upon the "researcher" and inside the "researcher". That's what makes life complicated when trying to take a Jungian standpoint and that's what makes life rich and fruitful even if sometimes it can be frightening when one finds parts of oneself while observing an "object" of whatever kind, specially if these are parts one was not aware of before. The face of No. 2 might differ widely from that of No. 1. And after all no one can be sure that there is no No. 3 or 4 or No … , still undiscovered and unheard.

With this in mind, it becomes obvious that it is neither an

exaggeration nor an empty phrase if we speak of an adventure we are in as soon we take the risks of really engaging with our "objects"(whether theoretical, clinical, artistic) because, basically, and in the end, our subjectivity is our main "object". To nourish, to evolve and bring life and structure is the way of individuation. What else is it all about?

Individuation means confrontation: confrontation with ambiguity, denseness, illusions, doubts, shadow. Most people have a solid aversion against all this. In at least one corner of our own hearts we want the world to be clear, organized, functioning, easy to understand, swift to handle and pleasant, and the snake to be in some other's garden. We want a kind of understanding that allows us to put all that is to know in a box and sell it in the market. This is the way of the *One-dimensional Man* as Herbert Marcuse named it. And it is the way of encrustment, decline and a fatal dereliction, the way to miss the chance of becoming a human being who is object and subject at the same time, and an individual who is affirming his *conditio humana*. Julian Green said: 'We never are, we are always becoming'.

So, let us take the chance to get involved again in the uncertain, the shimmering, the seducing new looks at old certainties. Let us get insecure to find new securities. As we will learn about fairy tales a little later: there is always a story behind the story, and a sense that in one, just as in the other, a contradistinction and – amidst that jumble – there is hope to find not just one single thread to lead us out, but something like a net or a mycelium to hold and nourish us in a more than one dimensional way and that might give us an idea of secureness in ambiguity. Maybe the secret of the Philosopher's Stone is that in fact it is liquid. At least sometimes.

So, let us dive into the morning, let us have a good and enriching time together.

Panel

How and Why We Still Read Jung:
Personal and Professional Reflections

Jean Kirsch

(USA, CGIJSF)

Introduction

Each of the four panel members represented here contributed an essay to a collection edited by Murray Stein and me, bearing the title *How and Why We Still Read Jung: Personal and Professional Reflections*. Contributors were encouraged to write about how they had developed a personally fulfilling and scholarly approach to reading and writing about Jung and why they continued to read him. As one might expect, widely diverse perspectives are represented in the book. We wanted the authors to write of their personal reading experience as well as offer their deep reading of Jung. Murray Stein and I regret that we could not have included more of the many strong writers in our field.

We hope that you are stimulated to reflect on your own reading of Jung. What keeps you coming back, time and again? What has inspired you to dig deeper in your own reading? Where do your passions lie and how do you nurture them? What unexpected opening will you discover today?

A Thank You: Some Brief Remarks and an Apology

Susan Rowland

(Pacifica Graduate Institute, USA)

(read by Jean Kirsch)

How and Why We Still Read Jung is a groundbreaking collection of essays edited by Jean Kirsch and Murray Stein. I am honored and delighted to be part of it. I thank Jean Kirsch, especially, for using her own voice to include me in this panel.

As a literature-trained academic without any clinical background, I once wrote a paper for the *Journal of Analytical Psychology* called, "Jung, the Trickster Writer, or What Literary Research can do for the clinician." The second part of the title was intended as an amusing aside, but the editors would not let me lose it in the process of publication. Now I see that this title speaks to my career-long involvement with Jungian psychology as having hidden connections with the humanities and "literary studies" in particular. In fact, my paper in this book, called "Reading Jung for Magic," now forms part of a book project using C. G. Jung and James Hillman to argue that Jungian psychology and literary studies share an unconscious and unwritten history.

One advantage of literary studies is the habit of reading in the mode of a quest: reading as asking what writing *is* or could be. When reading Jung for the first time, I found myself experiencing some of the pleasures frequently associated with creative writing, such as evocative symbols, mythical tropes, speculation, and humor. In particular, such "literary" devices neither appeared ornamental nor did they detract from the "psychology." Rather imaginative, dramatic, and symbolic writing proved fundamental to the psychology's expression.

Jung, I concluded, was intrinsically literary. I began to recognize that not only was his writing especially suitable to literary analysis, but also it *belonged* to literary categories. Above all, I saw that Jung's writing was responsive to reading as quest because it was *writing as quest*. Jung's work belonged to post-Romantic literature, when writing stopped being valued for its strict adherence to past models. Romantic works do not obey rules. Rather, Romantic writing is in search of the rules and theories by which it might be comprehended.

Here is writing that fulfills Romanticism's radical agenda. Jung's writing frees the reader's psyche from too narrow notions of rational truth. It does so by seeking knowledge as a quest for its rules rather than an enactment of them.

To me, Jung's writing is also a quest for meaning—a quest that embraces fictional, poetic, mythic, rhetorical, logical, and empirical strategies. Part of its quest nature is to address and unravel distinctions between science and art. Reading Jung is to engage the *whole* psyche since much of the so-called literary qualities invoke the "other," those parts of ourselves that modernity has sited/cited beyond the ego along our developmental path. It is in this spirit that I commend to this audience the rich reflections of this panel (and also my apologies that the back surgery I underwent this year prevents me from joining you!).

Jung Opens a Door to Another World

David Tacey

(La Trobe University, Melbourne, Australia)

When I was invited to write a chapter on "How and Why I Still Read Jung," I mentally ran through the major contributions of Jung's work and how they have impacted my life and thought. Numerous elements stood out, but I settled on the *symbolic attitude* as the element that brings me back to Jung time and again. Jung defines the symbolic attitude as one that "assigns meaning to events, whether great or small, and attaches to this meaning a greater value than to bare facts" (CW6, par. 819). It is an orientation to things of the inner and outer world which treats them symbolically rather than literally. As an intuitive thinker, this appealed to me, although I became aware that a fine line separates the symbolic attitude from paranoia, a condition in which meaning so overrides facts that the world is lost in an ocean of imputed meanings.

The symbolic attitude is an orientation to the contents of our experience that views them as pointing to, hinting at, another reality. I have always had a sense that another world runs parallel to this one. This has predisposed me to a love of poetry, music, mythology, and mysticism. Each of these discourses affirms that there is a level of reality, normally hidden, that we sometimes may access, especially through art and dream. That other parallel world Jung calls *psychic reality*. We normally live in the realm of external perceptions, but Jung opens the door to another world, which is not supernatural, as some of his critics maintain, but another way of viewing the natural, the world we already have. As Paul Eluard put it: "There is another world, but it is in this one."

In my view, we are desperately in need of this "other" world, but we are exiled from it by virtue of literal thinking and superficial readings of experience. Jung put it this way: "Humanity is in need of a symbolic life, badly in need. We only live banal, ordinary, rational or irrational things … but we have no symbolic life. Where do we live symbolically?" (CW18, par., 625).

Once upon a time, religion performed the task of delivering a symbolic life and nourishing the soul. But for the majority of people in the "enlightened" West, this is no longer the case. As a child, I did not live in the enlightened West, and thus I had a chance to participate in symbolic living. I grew up in a religious family, which was poor, uneducated, and unaware that the world outside the religious one was disenchanted. In a way, I value this upbringing, because although I eventually had to reject the naïve faith of my family, it at least got my symbolic life started. But I also grew up in central Australia, alongside the most ancient living civilization in the world, that of the Australian Aboriginals. Their lives were, and to some extent still are, steeped in the symbolic life, and as Jung once said, two-thirds of their conscious existence is lived in the symbolic realm (CW18, par. 649). Aboriginal Dreaming had a huge impact on my inner life, and predisposed my already intuitive mind to the symbolic domain.

I have to say that I gained more insight into symbolic reality from Aboriginal cultures than from my own European culture. Although devoutly Christian as a boy, I soon began to fall away from the kind of faith that was presented to me in childhood. I found it all, let us say, farfetched. Virgin births, physical resurrections, walking on water—all these miracles and wonders began to pall on me as I grew up and became more educated. By the time I was 15, I was hovering on the brink of atheism, although the Dreaming still worked on my soul. My shift toward atheism was hurried along at the age of 16 and 17 when, under the influence of my older sister, I was urged to read Nietzsche, Freud, and existential philosophers. She said our religious parents and family were out of touch with modernity and were 100 years behind the times.

At 18 years of age, I found the opportunity to go to university, funded by an academic scholarship, because my working-class father was opposed to education and said he would never give me "one cent" toward my tertiary studies. I entered my first year at university as a budding atheist, but it did not last long. Although no longer churchy, my faith began to resurface during the course of my studies, especially when I was introduced to the works of Jung in 1973. Jung was not on the curriculum; in fact, he was dismissed by my psychology tutor as a "discredited mystic." A chance meeting showed me the way. Molly Scrymgour, an old, humble, white-haired typist, whom the professors treated with disrespect, told me she "had a hunch" that I might take to Jung. Under her influence, I read through Molly's extensive personal library of Jung's writings and the entire secondary Jungian literature.

After completing my PhD degree, I won a postdoctoral award from the United States and was invited to select any professor in my field. I chose James Hillman in Dallas, although my sponsors in New York raised a protest, saying that "no good can come out of Texas." I worked academically with Hillman for a while, but in the course of our collaboration, he suggested that I would find out more about the unconscious if I went into analysis with him. Again, my sponsors were aghast! Becoming a patient was not what the Harkness Foundation had had in mind for me. Anyway, I talked them into letting me do this, and as soon as analysis got underway, up surfaced my dreams with Aboriginal motifs of initiation, rites of passage, and Dreaming themes.

After working with Hillman for a few years, I returned to Australia and, in 1995, wrote a book called *Edge of the Sacred,* because I felt that, after the analysis, I was hovering at the edge of a new kind of sacredness, one that seemed to want to burst out of my soul (Tacey, 1995/2009). It interested Hillman because it seemed to run parallel to his own preoccupation with Anima Mundi. The Aboriginal Dreaming made me aware, if only semiconsciously, that the world is not as it appears to the external senses, and that there is a huge dimension of reality that does not appear to those who see the world in literal terms. This theme, which Jung explores in "Mind and Earth," arguing that colonial people are impacted by the psychic lives of indigenous people, was difficult for me to express, because in my country a new code of political correctness had set in, which made venturing into Aboriginal spirituality problematical. It was seen as colonialist, exploitative, and opportunistic, so I received a lot of critical flack by daring to suggest that Aboriginal enchantment could actually serve to re-enchant the disenchanted souls of Westerners like myself.

What my critics failed to realize was that the "influence" of which I spoke was primarily unconscious borrowing, rather than conscious theft. It just happened, despite our politics. In a recent book, Astrid Berg discusses the same phenomenon from her African perspective (2012), and Roberto Gambini has discussed the same thing from his South American perspective (2003). Nevertheless, my *Edge of the Sacred* became a bestseller in my country, so obviously many of my compatriots were feeling the same way, even if it was intellectually controversial.

Meanwhile, Jung not only allowed me to understand what was happening to me on the inside regarding the indigenous world, but he also enabled me to reclaim my natal faith at a completely different level. His writings, especially *Answer to Job,* but also *Symbols of Transformation* and *Psychology and Religion,* enabled me to reclaim my Christian heritage in a way that the church itself could not allow. The church does not understand Jung's view because most of the people in it take their symbolic systems literally. For them, if something is stated in scripture, creed, or dogma, it is assumed to have occurred in space, time, and history, and to doubt this literal reading of scripture is to be cast out of the circle. Little wonder I had to throw out this version of faith by the time I reached adulthood. Jung casts all this literalism aside and shows us another way to appreciate the world of sacred discourse. In one sentence he put me on the right track regarding religion: "Considered from the standpoint of realism, the symbol is not of course an external truth, but it is psychologically true, for it was and is the bridge to all that is best in humanity" (CW5, par. 343).

This enabled me to reconnect with my Christian heritage in a life-changing way. Unfortunately, it also set me at odds with most others around me in the Christian community, for whom the symbolic approach is a heretical reduction of what they consider to be historical and factual truths. The last point I want to make is that reclaiming one's religious heritage is a kind of insurance against appropriating, and thus further devastating, the spiritual lives of indigenous peoples. The modern West is far less likely to act in predatorial ways toward the symbolic systems of indigenous peoples if it can find living symbolic content in its own traditions. If we can re-enchant our religious systems, this is good news for those who live in fear of what the Taos Pueblo chief described to Jung as the cruel hunger of white people: "Their lips are thin, their noses sharp, their faces furrowed … and they are always seeking something. What are they seeking?" (MDR, p. 276). They are seeking enchantment, of course, and having destroyed their own by literalism and rational thinking, they represent a great danger to those who are enchanted still.

Reflecting on Jung and Alchemy: A Daimonic Reading

Stanton Marlan

(USA, PSJA)

In the Jungian tradition, there are numerous ways of reading both Jung and alchemy. Jung's primary works and those of Marie-Louise von Franz, Edward Edinger, James Hillman, and Wolfgang Giegerich have been the most influential for me. All have contributed perspectives on how to read Jung and his alchemy. These are all strong and persuasive readings, and I read with them, through them, as well as against them, seeking my own perspective.

Harold Bloom has noted, "Reading well is best pursued as an implicit discipline; finally there is no method but yourself, when your self has been fully molded" (2000, p. 19). While I would never claim to be fully molded, my reading of Jung's alchemical works has been and continues to be fundamental to shaping my sense of self.

In a voice resonant to Bloom's, Giegerich has written: "… every potential reader has to try for himself to lift Jung's work and see what happens. No other person can do it for him" (1998, p. 60). For me, reading Jung's alchemy is heavy lifting. Reading alchemy in itself is by no means a benign quest. It is a *massa confusa* filled with impasses and dead ends, with shadows and suffering, and it resists unified intellectual summations and metanarratives. If I step back from Jung in my reading, it is less from what I believe Jung intended, than from the shadow of certain essentialist interpretations that have found their way into my understanding. By this, I mean readings that place emphasis on fixed and unchanging steps, structures, and static views of the archetypes, which minimize individual, cultural, and historical differences. Such interpretations reify a centralizing tendency and tend to become too easily encrusted, rock-hard representations of a dynamic psychic reality difficult to describe adequately in abstract form.

I have attempted to read Jung and alchemy with these reifying tendencies in mind. In many places, Jung likewise resisted the fixities of metanarratives and metaphysical constructions, and allowed himself to be carried along by the current of his experiences without knowing where they would lead.

This spirit sets the stage for what I call a daimonic reading, a reading that allows for the unknown edges of experience to remain open. Such openings allow for a greater range of imagination, for the fantastic that can decenter and destabilize our sense of the real and the line between fiction and truth. Walking this line is an opening to the unconscious, which can be a slippery slope of illusion and intoxication, a daimonic passion if not possession.

For me, reading daimonically is a kind of madness, a madness of allowing myself to be gripped and infected, to be carried by the flow into what feels like a phantasmagoria of alchemical fiction, a magical adventure that requires not only an engagement with Jung and alchemy, but also with my own depths, complexes, and daimones. To read in this way is to discover that in every reading there are multiple readers, others—"little people"—who have a say in the reading, at times even a story to tell.

I cannot silence my daimones who love alchemy. I identify with Jung's passion and with the alchemists in search of the Philosophers' Stone. I imagine such an identification as part inflation, part transference, part *participation mystique,* part fetish, and part poetic inspiration—a daimonic reading requires following the promptings of the unconscious "as if" it contains a meaningful *telos* that can shape our lives. For me, one such experience came in the form of a dream:

> I am in some kind of underground cavern. The atmosphere is Egyptian. I feel something deep in my chest start to rise up and fly out. It is a cat that is being resurrected from this Egyptian underworld. It is a numinous feeling, powerful and real. Organ music is playing, loud and resonant with the experience. A deep voice asks, "Who is John Dee?" and the dream comes to an end.

I had no personal association to the name John Dee. Years later, I learned of the English magus and alchemist John Dee (1527-1608), and reading about him gave me chills as I remembered my dream. Is it possible that my dream had any relationship to John Dee, the alchemist who was noted for his ability to converse with spirits? Is it possible that my dream reached beyond the subjectivity of time and place, connecting me to a transpersonal reality that was to become an important part of my future? Might one imagine that the dream question was asked by a daimon with a telos in mind? Perhaps such a reading of my dream is a wild fantasy, but Jung's understanding of the daimonic may give us pause:

> In so far as the archetypes do not represent mere functional relationships, they manifest themselves as "daimones," as personal agencies. In this form, they are felt as actual experiences and are not "figments of the imagination" as rationalism would have us believe (CW5, par. 388).

At the core of our personal complexes are archetypal realities, daimones of the objective psyche, which are not reducible to inner experiences. Jung recognized that these experiences did not spring from his conscious personality and so he called them "mana, daimon, or God. Science employs the term 'the unconscious,' thus admitting that it knows nothing about it ...." (MDR, p. 336).

The mystery of the daimon is as difficult to define as the unconscious. For me, the daimonic in reading, as in life, reflects the faces and forces of an unknown that interrupts the narrative force of the ego and points to an archetypal reality beyond it. As Jung famously remarked, "The decisive question for man is: Is he related to something infinite or not? That is the telling question of his life" (MDR, p. 325). I propose that this question can be answered positively to the extent that one has honored the daimones within.

Jung described his experience as "hitting upon a stream of lava," a fiery magma that burst forth from the unconscious and provided "the *prima materia* for a lifetime's work" (MDR, p. 199). Living so close to the fire can, however, lead to getting burnt. Daimonic reading and a daimonic life can be perilous, but for me, it is important to find the lava flow if my living is to also lead to illumination and to touch the soul.

One must turn toward the fire and engage it. Alchemical texts are replete with instructions about how to work with fire, and one learns how to do such work from within the fire itself. Hillman has noted, "The alchemist must be able to fight fire with fire, using his own fire to operate upon the fires with which he is operating. Working the fire by means of fire" (2010, p. 22). I believe this is the passion Jung originally brought to his inner life. In alchemy, the fire of Jung's active imagination was confirmed, and this connected him to the larger archetypal world he needed to advance his work.

In active imagination and in dreams, fantasy and identification can inflate us, but they can deflate us as well. On my first trip to Zürich many years ago, I saw Jung's house for the first time. I walked up the driveway, very excited to be close to Jung's spirit. I wanted an object, a material thing associated with Jung—even a stone to put on my desk to hold this spirit firm. I collected a few rocks from the ground and took them with me. I placed one on my desk and the others in a glass vessel. Through the stones, I felt I had a special connection to Jung, a *participation mystique*. When I touched these stones, the feeling of connection was reinforced. Jung and I were one in stone, a gift from psyche. My inevitable deflation came in the form of a dream:

> I am at the side door of Jung's house. I desperately want something of Jung's to take home with me. I knock and Emma Jung comes to the door. I explain who I am and tell her how important her husband is to me and ask her if there is anything of his she could give me. She says, "I'll be right back" and goes into the house. She returns and on the ground before me she places a pair of Jung's

shoes. With excitement, I step into them—only to discover they are far too big.

My first reaction to this humorous dream was utter deflation, but as time went on, its gift was the insight that Jung's shoes were not for me. This recognition led me to understand the problem of the *imitatio* of Jung: simply identifying with Jung was not the way to follow what the dream opened in my soul. Yet this recognition came on the heels of letting myself be carried by my daimonic spirit. With this recognition, I was able to relate to Jung's work in a more differentiated way. There was movement in my archetypal transference and a conscious response to it; the image of my small feet catalyzed a further development of my soul.

Every responsible active imagination also requires an ongoing engagement with one's daimones and a living dialogue with otherness and with our reading. Such a process often draws me down into my depths and out beyond them to the limits of my understanding. It relativizes my point of view and, in so doing, continues to open new horizons and to broaden my vision. It gives meaning to what initially appeared as nonsense and helps to deconstruct stale meanings. It opens a fertile abyss and connects me with a larger world and a sense of richness and substance. It is both inflating and deflating. So, if a daimonic reading is perilous, it is also for me an entrance to the treasure house of the soul.

Ambiguating Jung

Mark Saban

(UK, IGAP)

Memories, Dreams, Reflections is a strange and precious work. For me, doubts about its authenticity as Jung's autobiography have shown MDR to be even stranger and more precious than it hitherto seemed. It is now unveiled not only as a masterpiece (which it surely always was) but also as a masterpiece of ambiguity. In an important letter, Jung tells us that ambiguity "is superior to unequivocalness" because by doing "justice to the dual aspect of our psychic nature" it "reflects the nature of life" (1973a, pp. 69-70). This same ambiguity lends MDR its curious psychological depth, enabling it to perform both a negotiation with and an enactment of the divided nature of Jung's life. But my further contention is that it ultimately offers us a vantage point from which to re-vision the Collected Works and, therefore, his psychology as a whole.

As it happens, Jung didn't want his biography to be written by anyone, least of all himself. How could anyone "disentangle this monstrous Gordian knot of fatality, denseness and aspirations and what-not!" he asked. "I know too much about the impossibility of self-portrayal," he went on, "to want to venture on any such attempt" (MDR, p. viii). But eventually his resistance to the idea softened to ambivalence, and the project began. Quite apart from the ambiguities that inevitably shadow the genre of autobiography itself, equivocation was woven deeply into MDR and its making: It was to be written by Jung but also written by Aniela Jaffé; it was to be one of his books, but not one of the Collected Works; it was to be Jung's life, but only to be read after Jung's death.

Jung mistrusted autobiographies because they are full of what he called "self-deceptions and downright lies" (MDR, p. viii), but on the first page of MDR he simply states that the question of whether or not the stories that the book contains are true is simply not a problem: This book steps beyond truth or falsehood because it is the telling of a myth. And the myth it tells is Jung's "personal myth" (p. 3).

It is important to ensure that familiarity with this text doesn't soften the shockingly jarring impact of this paradoxical phrase: "personal myth," which was written long before Jungian and New Age books created an industry out of the idea. What is Jung talking about? If it is a myth, how can it be personal? How can the personal coincide with the mythic? In fact, this deliberate collision of the time-bound and the timeless, the general and the specific, was to characterize most of the stories Jung was to tell in MDR: "In the end the only events in my life worth telling" he says, "are those when the imperishable world irrupted into this transitory one" (MDR, p. 4).

What happened was that, despite himself, Jung became caught up in the unfolding of his childhood memories. Jaffé writes: "[S]omething so wonderful and meaningful happened… Jung himself is writing his autobiography all over again… so much had become clear to [Jung] and especially the meaning of his life which he had apparently not seen to its full extent" (Bair, 2004, p. 595).

In these early chapters of MDR, Jung persistently, almost obsessively, revisits images and ideas of divided identity: from Jung the child sitting on his stone and wondering if he were sitting on the stone or if he were the stone on which he sat, to the parental binary and its tensions—the uncanny mother in touch with numinosities of the night versus the desiccated diurnal spirituality of father. Eventually, however, this theme of duality coheres into the twin shape of his twofold personalities in all their dialectical complexity.

There are three important things to say about this psychic division.

First, it is never fully resolved. As Jung says, "The play and counterplay between personalities No. I and No. 2 ... has run through my whole life" (MDR, p. 45). Second, not only is it nonpathological, Jung insists, it is "played out in every individual" (p. 45): that is to say, it is a given, a fundamental of psychological existence. And third, Jung deliberately chooses to avoid the terminology of classical analytical psychology when describing the two personalities. He seems to want to place them (like MDR itself) outside of the structured psychology of the Collected Works; he is looking back, re-visioning, and even de-stabilizing his own work.

This personal creation myth of Jung's, this tale of the two personalities, is a concrete example of "the imperishable world irrupt[ing] into this transitory one" (MDR, p. 4). Personality I, which is broadly characterized by finitude, sameness, and limitation, is again and again disrupted by personality 2, which brings with it the unbounded, the Other, and the irrational. But crucially, the irreducible otherness of personality 2 is never, *and can never be,* integrated or contained by personality I, or vice versa. Hence Jung's emphasis upon the *interminable* nature of their oscillation within his life.

Like the Shakespeare comedy that always ends with a wedding, the familiar narrative of symmetry and synthesis that we find in the Collected Works, has a *telos* that is always *coniunctio.* But *this* plot is different. The mythos that the posthumous Jung offers us is one of Heraclitean war without end—unresolvable lifelong conflict: "The opposites and the contradictions between them do not vanish. They constantly threaten the unity of the personality, and entangle life again and again in their dichotomies" (MDR, p. 346).

MDR presents us with a psyche that consists of two, equally necessary, but entirely incompatible "personalities." One of them binds us to *this* life, *this* body, *this* limited set of possibilities, *this* limited range of conceptual expression. The other flings us out into radical alterity. It challenges our limits, dissolves our boundaries, and situates itself beyond our ability to express it in rational terms. *Neither of the personalities can be reduced to the other; neither is more "real" nor more "fundamental" than the other.* In MDR, neither No. I nor No. 2 is ever described as inferior or subservient to the other. But the myth tells us again and again that when Jung attempts to live *exclusively* in the realm of either No. I or No. 2 he fails to flourish as a human being. What we learn is that, ultimately, incompatible though they are, both personalities ask somehow to be inhabited.

The myth offers us an image of lived ambiguity. The psyche dwells in two contradictory realms, and psychic life consists in the difficult, all but impossible, negotiation of that fact.

Now let us return to our theme of reading. What happens if we allow this insight to inform the way in which we read Jung's opus?

My guess is that Jung is telling us that we need to do some difficult psychological work when we read his writings. The hard work in question is the labor of ambiguation. It entails reading his words as ambiguous, even when they seem univocal. In fact, *especially* when they seem univocal. It means awakening to the voice of whichever personality is least audibly present at any one time, and trying to catch, behind what is most explicit in the text, that trace of the Other which haunts it, like a barely heard harmonic overtone. "Everything I have written has a double bottom," said Jung (von Franz, 1975, p. 4).

We can see why, late in life, Jung was drawn to the radical polysemy of alchemy. There he could bypass the classification and conceptualization of what is, by its nature, beyond containment. Finally, he could write a psychology that did justice to the endless dialectic of the psyche. Simultaneously concrete and ambiguous, his language could and did reflect and amplify the duality of the two personalities: *ora et labora*.

Of course, the opus of psychotherapy (an opus that always backgrounds Jung's manifest focus, whatever it may be) requires a style of engagement strikingly similar to that of the ambiguous reading I have been attempting to describe. In the consulting room, therapist reads patient and patient reads therapist in a highly complex reciprocal dance that, for all its spontaneity, pulsates to an ongoing rhythm of intertwined pattern and chaos. Points of certainty and limitation in both patient and therapist require constant dissolution, and patches of vagueness and confusion perpetually need to be coalesced: *solve et coagula*. The transformative nature of the process requires mutuality, though it would be naïve and unrealistic to assume that it is perfectly symmetrical. Between and within these dynamics the eccentric interplay of same and Other is disclosed: within and between both therapist and patient. This is the same dialectical relation that Jung describes in his evocation of the two personalities in MDR, though on a different register.

MDR shows us how the coexistence of two personalities throughout Jung's life and work, and the resulting oscillation between them, ultimately enables a vision of psyche as a region of irreducible ambiguity. The ambiguity presents itself not only in the *content* of MDR, but also in its form and its origin. In the light of the double-vision offered within this realization, we, his readers, are implicitly encouraged to return to the Collected Works, and, as it were, re-ambiguate those aspects of his writing that have undergone an inevitable sedimentation into singleness of meaning and calcification into rigidity of structure. This reading requires us to remain open to the difficulties and the potencies that co-inhere within our divided natures, and allow the "play and counterplay" to be sustained—even within that double-reading.

Finally, this is what is most challenging, but also most worthwhile about this project—this attempt to revive and re-vision the complex and irregular interweaving of Jung's No. 1 with No. 2. It cannot be achieved at a distance, but only through a *further* interweaving, whereby we entwine our own doublings into Jung's and hence collude in his opus, which thereby necessarily also becomes our own.

Bibliography

Bair, D. (2004). *Jung : A Biography*. London: Little, Brown.

Berg, Astrid (2012). *Connecting with South Africa: Cultural Communication and Understanding*. College Station, TX: Texas A & M University Press.

Bloom, H. (2000). *How to Read and Why*. New York: Simon and Shuster.

Gambini, Roberto. (2003). *Soul and Culture*. College Station, TX: Texas A & M University Press.

Giegerich, W. (1998). *The Soul's Logical Life: Towards a Rigorous Notion of Psychology*. Berlin: Peter Lang Publishing.

Hillman, J. (2010). *Alchemical Psychology,* Uniform Edition, Vol. 5. Putnam, CT: Spring Publications.

Jung, C. G. (1912/1952). *Symbols of Transformation*. In *The Collected Works of C. G. Jung*, Vol. 5. (Gerhard Adler, Ed.; R.F.C. Hull, Trans.). Princeton: Princeton University Press.

— (1921/1971). "Definitions: Symbol" *Psychological Types*. CW6.

— (1939). *The Symbolic Life*. CW18.

— (1963/1995). *Memories, Dreams, Reflections*. Recorded and edited by Aniela Jaffé. London: HarperCollins.

— (1973a). *Letters, Vol. 2*. Princeton, N.J.: Princeton University Press.

Tacey, David. (1995). *Edge of the Sacred: Transformation in Australia*. Melbourne: HarperCollins. Republished in a revised international edition as *Edge of the Sacred: Jung, Psyche, Earth*. Einseideln, Switzerland: Daimon, 2009.

von Franz, M.-L. (1975). *C. G. Jung: His Myth in Our Time*. New York: Published by Putnam for the C. G. Jung Foundation for Analytical Psychology.

The Double Coniunctio Tales

Pia Skogemann

(Denmark, DSAP)

Interpreting Fairy Tales

The interpretation of fairy tales has been a part of the Jungian treasure box from Jung's lifetime, most of all because in fairy tales we have access to the possibility of using them to help foster the under-standing and development of symbolic attitude. Fairy tales describe psychological processes in a symbolic form. They can be used to understand life processes that have gone stale, as fairy tale patterns can be used as a way to renew those processes.

Many modern Jungians have tried out their theoretical ideas by applying them to fairy tales in one way or another. In many Jungian training programs, the candidates are asked to write essays involving the interpretation of fairy tales, so it is important that we have a frame that can act as a guide when an interpretation is most needed.

Traditionally, one would look to Marie-Louise von Franz, who introduced the classical Jungian method for interpreting fairy tales. Von Franz (1995) recommended that in the beginning and at the end of a fairy tale we take into account the number of persons and their gender to identify motifs and archetypal images and pay attention to the meaning of all the symbols in their context. Finally, she found it important to compare one fairy tale with similar fairy tales.

Structuring Fairy Tales

I continue to find her framework very useful. However, I would like to offer you another way of *structuring* fairy tales. While several Jungians have discussed other aspects of fairy tales, since Von Franz, no one has discussed their structure. She used Aristotle's dramaturgic model for Greek tragedy; that is a setting of the stage, one or more complications, a turning point and a *lysis*. I believe that fairy tales are more narrative than dramatic in their structure. This is because their origins are in the oral tradition, while the classical theatre has a literary tradition.

I have been looking for a sequential, structural pattern in the narratives, and what I have found fits a large number of fairy tales. (Skogemann1998).

The Double Coniunctio Tales

The model has 2x4 sequences, both ending with a *Coniunctio.* The structuring is like the syntactic grammar of a sentence; the sequences appear in a definite order as sections of a narrative.

Donald Kalsched (1996, p. 146ff) also speaks about two *Coniunctios* in fairy tales, but his intention is different from mine, as he is looking for specific examples of how a traumatized ego is healed, and not for a general structure pattern in fairy tales as such. Not all fairy-tale egos are traumatized, and not all of Kalsched's examples involve two *Coniunctios* in the way I use the term.

Just as we distinguish little dreams from big dreams, I think we also can distinguish "little" fairy tales from "big" fairy tales. Little fairy tales can have many facets; some are for children, some are just meant to be funny or frightening or even obscene, and then there is the large group of One Coniunctio tales with 4 sequences and Double Coniunctio tales with 8 sequences. The Double Coniunctio pattern has existed from as long back as Amor and Psyche, and it appears in a great number of fairy tales. In my opinion, only this latter group should be thought of as big fairy tales, in that they describe an individuation pattern in the classical Jungian sense.

The 8-sequence model - overview

o 1. Background   o 5. Crisis

o 2. Outward impulse   o 6. Loss and Isolation

o 3. Detachment   o 7. Achievement

o 4. First Conjunctio   o 8. Second Conjunctio

Figure I

The 8-Sequence Model

1. Background

This is usually about the parents of the hero(ine). This sequence indicates the parental problems, often also gives some information about the hero(ine)'s conception, their birth and childhood events. This background is what shapes the pattern of the hero(ine)'s life. The background sequence can be very long and detailed or very short, like a message – for instance, it may just mention a stepmother.

2. Outward Impulse

This is the impulse which initiates the development of the hero(ine). It is a longing that leads him/her away from home, and more or less hidden in it is the longing for the unknown Other. It happens to a young person, typically 15 years old, if an age is mentioned.

3. Detachment

To this sequence belongs the journey out into the world. If the previous stage was determined by an impulse, a wish, a longing or a dream, in this sequence we see the doings of an active ego. This is the first detachment from the parental world.

4. First Coniunctio

What happens here is the erotic encounter with the other sex. Often it happens in an illegitimate way: maybe the parents don't know about it and, even if marriage takes place, the marriage will have to be repeated in the second Coniunctio at the end of the fairy tale. The couple's relationship is still shrouded in a cloud of projections.

5. Crisis

The encounter of the couple, or their living together; sometimes they even have children together; this is followed by some kind of regressive crisis. Maybe one of the couple is longing to see their home again; they visit the parents and receive advice which provokes a separation from the loved one. Or another common motive: the mother-in-law or the stepmother interferes in the relationship in various destructive ways, also resulting in separation.

6. Isolation and Loss

The separation makes the abandoned lover conscious of her/ his love and initiates a search for the lost love. Often, there are long wanderings and severe trials and humiliations, but also helpful encounters and magical devices, before the seeker comes close to the lover again.

7. Achievement and Victory

But the difficulties are not over yet. Although the seeker has found out where the lover is and the lover is now close, he/she is often about to marry another. The lover has to see through all disguises and recognize who their true partner is. The lover has to show that he/she reciprocates the seeker's love and chooses the true love. Often, there is also a final resolution of the negative parental complex.

8. The Second Coniunctio

The couple marry or remarry, in a standard happy ending. The essential thing is that their union is on new and mutual terms. It is a symbol of a successful individuation pattern. In his latest work (2013, p. 310), Donald Kalsched offers an interpretation of *The Woman without Hands* where our two approaches actually coincide: "The first marriage was a rescue from without – what alchemy describes as a lesser Coniunctio…The second marriage is a true wedding of equals on the common ground of each partner's wholeness. The new union is what alchemy describes as the greater Coniunctio".

Defining the Method for Structuring the Double Coniunctio Tales

A: The two *Coniunctios* are the most important of the eight sequences, and the first ones to look for. Although a few of the other sequences might be missing, the tale may still belong to this group. All such tales are rich tales, describing patterns of individuation. I should add that folklore research has shown that the primary audience of such tales was adults, not children (Skogemann, 1998, p. 15).

B: The main character is seen as an archetypal ego-model and is followed through the fairy tale as a person, whether male or female. The lover is the secondary main character.

C: The model allows for different ways of being feminine or masculine – just as the main male character is seen as an archetypal ego, so is the female. Female agency is seen as natural in a woman's psyche, just as empathic qualities are seen as natural in a man's psyche. If one of the lovers, male or female, is the more active one, the other tends to be more passive. Either way, the one who is initially the active one is usually the passive one after the first *Coniunctio*.

D: When the process involving this structure is complete, interpretation can be carried through guided by the structure. For the interpretation it is important to evaluate the maturity of the ego versus the degree of initial traumatization.

E: Other Jungian approaches of interpretation can then be added, such as specific symbolic/archetypal themes (Jung, 1945), comparing with other variants (Von Franz, 1995) and/or specific clinical themes (Asper, 1987, Kast, 1993, Kalsched, 1996; 2013, Dieckmann, 1997). It is important to note that the structuring is not in itself a full interpretation.

An Example of a Danish Fairy Tale, Published in 1881

The Prince's Plumage

Once upon a time there was a princess who was in love with a prince, but this her stepmother did not like. The stepmother told the King that she was afraid that the sweetheart would seduce the princess. The King decided to build a house for the princess on a small island in the sea, with a pontoon bridge so that they could visit her. When the pontoon bridge was ashore, neither the prince nor anyone else could visit the princes. She was sent out to the island with just a maid to serve her .The stepmother's own daughter, however, was to remain in the King's castle.

But soon the princess's sweetheart got the news of her whereabouts. He had a pair of wings made, and he flew out to her as often as they both liked.

Whenever the stepmother visited the princess, she found her happy and cheerful. The stepmother suspected the reason for this and decided to send her own daughter out on the island to spy on the princess. The stepsister soon heard the princess's sweetheart flying and bashing his wings against the windows.

Of course she told her mother of her discovery, and they wanted to put an end to the visits. The stepsister was sent out again, this time with a knife. She was going to damage the lover's wings so that he would fall into the sea and drown. But the princess was alert, and when her lover came and her stepsister cut his wings with the knife, the princess took hold of him, so he did not fall. They tried to repair the wings, so he could get away. But the worst of all was that they could never speak a word to each other without her stepsister hearing them.

Because his wings were now damaged, the princess's sweetheart was not sure that he could make it back across the sea. But he would give the princess a sign: if he crossed over safely, the sea would be clear, but if he did not, it would be blood-red.

He also gave the princess three rings: one for her waist, one for her arm and the third one for her finger. They were designed so that when he became betrothed to a new girlfriend, the ring around the princess's waist would break; when he ate with his new betrothed, the ring around the princess's arm would break, and when he danced with her, the ring on the princess's finger would break.

The stepsister heard about the sea turning blood-red, and when she returned to her mother, they busied themselves slaughtering animals. They filled an entire tub with blood which they poured into the sea below the princess's windows. They wanted her to believe that her lover had drowned.

The princess saw the blood, but she was not convinced that her lover had in fact drowned. It may well be a deception, she thought. She spoke with her maid about it, and they planned to give a feast for her parents and stepsister. And so they did. The guests came and the princess gave them a lot to drink and eat, acting in a most charming and cheerful way, while the maid packed away their belongings. When the princess saw that the guests had become somewhat merry, she and the maid sneaked out onto the floating bridge and crossed over it. They then took the bridge ashore and left the others on the island.

And they may still be there today.

Now the princess and her maid changed into men's clothes, and went to the castle, where her lover came from, pretending to be marksmen. It turned out that the princess's lover was betrothed and soon to be wed to another woman. They needed a lot of game for the wedding feast and had good use for marksmen. The princess and her maid were hired and went out hunting. They always had good luck, and some people said that they must be female marksmen, since they had such luck. This should be tested, they said. They would sprinkle peas on the stairs up to the chamber where the marksmen were sleeping. When the marksmen stepped on the peas and stumbled, if they were women they would flinch and scream, but if they were men, they would just walk on.

A little boy heard what was agreed and went and told the princess and her maid that people thought they were female marksmen. "But you can always carry your slippers in your hands and run barefoot" he said. "Then you will not stumble."

The princess and her maid thanked the boy and followed his advice. And they were not found out.

When the day of the wedding came, the ring around the princess's waist broke. As they all sat down to eat, the ring on her arm broke and fell into the bridegroom's plate. He grabbed it and said, "This is mine."

When the dance began, the ring on the princess's finger broke. This one she wanted to keep, but it broke just at the moment when, during the dance, the princess, still in a marksman's clothes, handed over to the prince his fiancé, and then he recognized her. He told everyone that the princess was his former betrothed. He said goodbye to the other woman, and then he married the princess and they lived happily ever after.

Structuring and a Short Interpretation

As my main interest here is to demonstrate the method of structuring and its implications, I will not go deeply into the symbolic interpretations our fairy tale. Along the way I will compare this tale with *Cinderella,* a fairy tale so well known that I assume you will be able to follow even without a resume. You will then see how the same structure can be applied to very different tales.

1. Background

In our fairy tale there is no background story explicitly told, other than that there is a stepmother and a stepsister. From this it can be inferred that the princess's mother is dead. The background section in fairy tales can be very long and often is.

By comparison, in *Cinderella* we are told in detail how the mother became ill and made Cinderella promise that she will always be good and gentle, how the father remarried, and how the two stepsisters bullied Cinderella. We are also told how the father went to the market having offered to bring home presents for the girls, and how Cinderella asked for a hazel branch which she planted on her mother's grave and watered it with her tears until it grew high, and a white bird sat in its branches, so when Cinderella uttered a wish for something, the bird would drop it down to her.

2. Outward Impulse

Falling in love is a mighty outward impulse. This is the actual beginning of our fairy tale's narrative. The stepmother does not like it, and probably wants to prevent the prince proposing to the princess, because she wants her own daughter to be the object of his desire.

In *Cinderella*, the outward impulse appears with her wish to go to the ball at the castle, with the purpose of winning the prince. This is denied her by the stepmother who appears quite sadistic when she promises Cinderella that she may go to the ball if she performs this and that impossible task – but when she does complete them all, she is still scornfully denied her wish to go to the ball.

3. Detachment

In *The Prince's Plumage,* the princess is sent away to live by herself on the island with only her maid. The stepmother thinks she controls the access to the princess. But in reality, the princess wins much more freedom than she would have had, had she remained in her father's home.

Cinderella gets fantastic dresses from the bird in the magical hazel tree, she goes to the ball and returns home in secret.

4. First Coniunctio

The prince soon comes to the princess disguised as a bird. Using a bird's plumage as a means of transport is frequent in Scandinavian mythology and folklore. Freya, the Love Goddess, was known to use it, and she could lend it to other gods.

Clearly, the love affair between the princess and the prince is now realized, but in an illegitimate way.

In *Cinderella*, this sequence is covered by the three balls at the King's castle, where the prince only dances with Cinderella and claims that she is "his lady".

A number of fairy tales simply end with the first Coniunctio and marriage straight away. In those instances it usually makes good sense to see the core issue as relating to (one of) the parents and their background – the hero(ine) is not yet in the more mature relationship to a partner. One might also say that the first four sequences are about growing up, while the next four of the eight sequences involve the anima/animus and the withdrawal of projections and the maturation of the relationship to the Self and Other – that is individuation in the classical Jungian sense.

A well-known example of a One Coniunctio tale is *Briar Rose*. The background sequence takes up the first half of the tale, explaining the Queen's difficulties in conceiving; then the terrible anger of the 13th uninvited wise-woman who casts a death-spell on the little girl which is only partly averted by the last wise-woman. The outward impulse makes the princess explore the whole castle when she is alone for the first time, at the age of fifteen. Here, she meets the old woman, pricks her finger on the spindle and falls under the 100-year spell of sleep. When the 100 years are over, the prince walks right through the hedge, finds her and kisses her, and they marry.

Among feminists (for example Rowe, 1986), fairy tales have acquired quite a negative reputation, mainly because the most well-known fairy tale heroines such as Briar Rose, Little Red Riding Hood, and Snow White are so childlike and passive. This is really not a fault of the fairy tales as such, but rather the selection and editing, especially by the Grimm Brothers.

5. Crisis

The stepsister is so close that she can hear every word the lovers say to each other, we are told. We could easily interpret the stepsister as a shadow part of the princess – meaning that a lover's quarrel is separating the couple so that the prince leaves in pain from his damaged wing. If the relationship is to continue, some projections have to be taken back, and both partners must commit to each other on a deeper level.

The regression that is always involved in this sequence must not be viewed from a causal point of view, but from a final point of view. According to Jung (CW 8, par. 43) "according to the concept of finality, causes are understood as means to an end."

In *Cinderella* there is no crisis sequence as such. The lovers *are* already separated – at the end of each ball at the castle, Cinderella runs away and hides in the ashes in the kitchen.

6. Loss and Isolation

The stepmother and stepsister try to make the princess believe that her sweetheart is dead. However, she does not believe them. Instead, she tricks the family to drink too much and simply leaves them behind on the isolated island. This is a heroine who, unlike Cinderella, is not always good and gentle.

Ashore, the princess and her maid take on a male disguise as marksmen. When in fairy tales the heroine is about to do something out of her traditional gender role, she will often put on men's clothes. This is not about identifying with the animus.

When the two young women arrive at the prince's castle, it is only to learn that he is about to marry another woman. This is a very common motif; in many instances, the prince is even under a spell, as in the *Beauty and the Beast* variants. So, the princess has to keep up the male disguise, shooting game and biding her time.

We see here an example of the point I made at the beginning of the paper – here the prince was the active one in the first part of the tale, and now the situation is reversed; the princess has shown strong self-agency by outwitting the stepmother and finding the prince.

In *Cinderella*, she was the (relatively) active one in the first part of the narrative using all her resources to meet the prince and win him. Now she has to wait in silence while he is looking for her, testing all the young ladies with her own lost shoe, even her stepsisters who cut their toe and heel to fit in her shoe.

7. Achievement

The three magical rings that the prince had given the princess can only do their job in the last moments of the enfolding events. During the dance, (the princess is still in male clothes) the ring on her finger breaks when she passes on to the prince his new fiancée, and then he finally recognizes her. Magical rings can, of course, mean many things, but in this case I think they represent the feelings which the prince invested in the princess when they were together on the island. Now his feelings return to him, and he recognizes her as his true love.

Again, by comparison, in *Cinderella*, the prince recognizes Cinderella just after he sees that the shoe fits her.

8. Second Coniunctio

The prince explains to everybody that the princess was his original fiancée, and they marry. The false bride is sent home.

In *Cinderella*, the two stepsisters are severely punished after the wedding, and their eyes are picked out by the birds.

I hope I have demonstrated to you that my 8-sequence model works for very different fairy tales; one with a rather active and industrious heroine, and the other with Cinderella as the ever good and gentle heroine.

Snow White and the Seven Dwarfs

Applying my structure model to fairy tales, which have traditionally been interpreted as individuation tales, will sometimes reveal that they are not. *Snow White* has had an almost iconic status since Disney created the first animated film based on it in 1937. Helen M. Arnold presented a Jungian interpretation with the subtitle "A Symbolic Account of Human Development" (1979). More recently, this view has been modified: Stephen Flynn published a paper on *Snow White* on The Jung Page (2005) describing what is, in his opinion, "the immature feminine psyche", and Jutta von Buchholtz, wrote a paper published on www.jungatlanta.com (2007) entitled "She was quite a ninny, wasn't she?" (A ninny being a very stupid person).

If we apply the model I have developed here, we can throw a new light on *Snow White and the Seven Dwarfs* as it is told in the Grimm version. Through most of the story, the heroine is a child, just seven years old. It seems that she becomes a young woman while appearing dead in the glass coffin. The motif of the glass coffin, in my opinion, shows a seriously traumatized ego, not an introverted individuation phase. There is only one Coniunctio – a marriage with a stranger.

It is true that many real princesses in the history of Europe suffered a similar fate – being treated as non-persons until they were ready to breed, and then traded off into a marriage with some foreign prince. But this is not what we usually think of as an individuation pattern.

However, in comparison with other versions of *Snow White*, I suspect that the Grimm brothers must take responsibility for some serious editorial distortion in the narrative pattern.

In other – Danish – versions that I have read, Snow White is a young woman, and she does have a relationship with the prince before she is exiled into the forest. In a couple of versions, she is even pregnant. Walt Disney casted the heroine into a very traditional gender role as a sweet girl only longing for true love, but as a teenager, not a child, and she and the prince meet in the beginning and fall in love with each other. In the end, the prince deliberately searches for her after freeing himself from the prison of the evil Queen. I think that Disney may have made these changes intuitively, to create a more satisfactory narrative structure. That is, changes that make the narrative fit into the Double Coniunctio group of fairy tales.

Conclusion

I hope that I have succeeded in demonstrating the relevance and helpfulness of applying a narrative structure to fairy tales. I can compare the structure model with a loom set up for weaving, and the individual fairy tale with the warp and weft. All kinds of motifs, colors and patterns may emerge from the same kind of loom; but they are bound to appear in a certain sequence, and they have a direction towards an aim. The model is connected with process, finality and maturation of relationship, not with plot or symbolic content.

The model has clinical relevance too, especially if you are already comfortable with the use of fairy tales and fairy tale motifs in your therapy style. My own clinical approach is similar to what Dieckmann describes in *Fairy-tales in psychotherapy* (1997) – taking notes of fairy tale motifs in dreams and fantasies, asking patients about their favorite fairy tale or even suggesting a fairy tale for them to read. In most of Dieckmann's examples, however, the initial phase of the therapy coincides with a motive from the beginning of a fairy tale, i.e. the Background sequence. He does not address the later stages. What my model can add is help in keeping track of the progress of therapeutic process. When fairy tale motives emerge later in the therapy, they typically belong to one of the later parts in the narrative structure. And a regressive crisis in therapy could very well mark the beginning of an individuation process, corresponding with the crisis sequence.

Bibliography

Asper, K. (1993). *The Abandoned Child Within: On Losing and Regaining Self-Worth*. New York: Fromm International Publishing Corporation.

Dieckmann, H. (1997). Fairy Tales in psychotherapy. *Journal of Analytical Psychology*, 42:2, 253-268.

Jung, C. G. (1945). *The Phenomenology of the Spirit in Fairy Tales* CW 9i, 384-455.

Jung, C. G. (1948). *On Psychic Energy*. CW 8, 23.

Kalsched, D. (1996). *The Inner World of Trauma*. London and New York: Routledge, Kalsched, D. (2013). *Trauma and the Soul*. London and New York: Routledge.

Kast, V. (1993). *Through Emotions to Maturity: Psychological Readings of Fairy Tales*. New York: Fromm International Publishing Corporation

Rowe, Karen E. (1986). Feminism and Fairy Tales. *Don't Bet on the Prince*. New York: Routledge.

Skogemann, P. (1998). *En Karl var min mor, en fisk var min far*. Copenhagen: L & R Fakta.

von Franz, M.-L. (1995). *The Interpretation of Fairy Tales*. Boston: revised Version, Shambala.

Wednesday, 21 August 2013

Introduction

Pilar Amezaga

Master of Ceremonies

(Uruguay, SUPA)

It gives me great pleasure to welcome you to what is to be the third day of the Congress. We have now reached the halfway stage of what is turning out to be a banquet of ideas that reflect creativity, diversity, development and evolution; all emanating from Jungian thought. For two days now we have been sharing our experiences, our way of thinking, our doubts and our differing realities. Today we will not only be learning about the application of Jungian principles in a group setting but also finding out what Eros is capable of achieving within two communities of an entirely different nature.

This morning you will be invited to hear, as I understand it, two manifestations of Eros. First, you will hear Eduardo Carvallo and Eva Pattis Zoja telling us about the work they have been carrying out in Colombia with a group of children who find themselves in an extremely vulnerable situation, followed by Gianni Nagliero and Vito Marino de Marinis exploring the different routes that could lead to a resolution of the conflict that exists between Jungian Societies in Italy.

Although they both have a different dream as a starting point, they have a common denominator in Eros and in the search for Agape and Philia; for solidarity; for respect and the acknowledgement of the need for openness and convergence. One is a dream based on the desire to improve the social standing of those living in poverty and the need to lighten the isolation of the consulting room while the other is a dream hoping for reencounter, openness, exchange and reconciliation.

Both presentations invite us to reflect on the obligations we have as a community to continue to grow and to create new roads that will help us build a better future.

It is my hope that after listening to these two presentations you too will feel the same degree of optimism that I did after reading them to give this brief introduction. Our community is made up of people who are not passive or indifferent when facing struggle, pain or suffering either at a social or institutional level. These two presentations once again confirm my belief that our profession and the values that we hold dear as analysts lead us to become better persons. They allow us to escape our egocentric selves, to grow and to better individualize ourselves.

In both presentations I perceived a need to meet with the other despite the differences. There is a need for exchange, for solidarity and respect, and this need is capable of building new roads that can transform the pain of isolation.

Both presentations break new ground, taking Jungian action and thought to a social level and to the realm of groups. They defy us to venture into new realities that clearly transcend the everyday reality of our consulting rooms and our individual analysis.

Both presentations are also controversial. In the first, Sandwork: An Experience Of Working With The Colombian Vulnerable Population, we see a way of working which is far removed from the individual work done in a consulting room, while in the second: From Splits to Collaboration: The Process of Resolving Conflicts between Societies, we are shown how a conflict in Italy, resulting from the different interpretations of Jungian thought embodied in different Jungian societies, is resolved.

If I were asked to describe how these two new projects originated, I would look towards Eros as the starting point that provides impulse and nobility, an Eros that sustains them and provides them with the initiative to bring something new to share with all of us. Let us share this encounter and this experience with them.

Expressive Sandwork:
An Experience of Working with Colombian Vulnerable Population

Eduardo Carvallo

(Colombia, SVAJ)

Eva Pattis Zoja

(Italy, ÖGAP/CIPA)

We would like to thank the Scientific Committee of this Congress for the opportunity to share this time with you. We feel privileged to do so.

The Importance of Incorporating Social Work in Psychotherapy

What we will be presenting is the result of teamwork we have developed over the last ten years, thanks to the efforts and dedication of a group of generous volunteers, Jungian analysts and IAAP routers from different countries and continents, some of whom are with us here today. (Please, could you raise your hands those of you who are here so that everyone can see a small part of our team).

Very slowly, in the last ten years, we have built a methodology that we have called "Expressive Sandwork" – a trans-cultural, non-verbal tool that has been an effective psycho-social support for children in situations where individual psychotherapy has not been possible.

This approach may appear unusual for two reasons: it is based on Jungian concepts applied to social life, and it is related to group processes.

In a James Hillman's article entitled "From the Mirror to the Window: Curing Psychoanalysis of its Narcissism", he mentions that psychoanalysis needs to pay attention to social problems. He gets us to reflect on the fact that while analysts and their patients have remained looking at each other in the mirror for a long time, in the outer world there is a society that has been desperately waiting.

Since then, the way we understand our profession has changed a great deal. Today, approaching Hillman's proposition, we could say that we need to move again, and this time not only from the mirror to the window, but from the window to the door.

We need to open our psychoanalytical consulting rooms, reconsider our individual settings and our theoretical concepts. We need to get our hands a little bit dirty.

This reminds us of Freud's position when in 1918 he talked for the first time about a plan to open sessions, with no cost, to treat people in need who could not afford a psychoanalytical treatment.

This social vision of Psychoanalysis was established with the "Free Clinics" in Vienna and Berlin, which worked between 1920 and 1933 until they disappeared during the Nazi regime.

Some 100 years later, Expressive Sandwork sees itself as a small contribution to this vision, in a world that has undergone enormous changes.

Contextualization of the Experience

Defining Vulnerable Communities

In many of the regions we live in, we co-habit with people who live in very precarious conditions. Collective groups that are exposed to conditions that threaten their members biologically, psychologically and spiritually, interfering with their natural capacity for development and adaptation – these are the so-called vulnerable communities.

These conditions mainly affect children, who are exposed to drugs, violence, sexual abuse and other experiences that their psychobiological system is not prepared to assimilate.

Colombia: A "Sample" Country

The experience we share today was developed in Colombia.

In spite of the fact that its economic indexes place it among the developing countries, as are most Latin American countries, Colombia's poverty levels are very high.

Official 2012 figures reveal that 10.5% of the general population are at extreme poverty levels. This means that their income does not reach USD 1.50 per day.

As a way of evading their reality, many members of these communities resort to consuming low cost psychoactive drugs.

The presence of brain damage among these people is often responsible for their impulsive and aggressive behaviour that permanently affect the physical integrity of the rest of the community members and especially the children.

Beside these conditions, shared by practically every poverty-stricken community around the world, in Colombia there are two phenomena caused by an unconventional warfare that has existed there for over 50 years: community displacement and heavy criminality among teenagers known as hit men.

In Colombia, entire communities decide to abandon their land, their properties and ways of earning their living because of the threat of death due to the confrontations between the Government Armed Forces and the Guerrillas or Paramilitary Forces; or as has happened on several occasions, after suffering massacres perpetrated by these latter groups, who have accused them of complicity and being "informers" of the enemy.

In 2011, Colombia came to the top of the world list of countries with the most displaced victims enforced by armed conflict: 5.2 million inhabitants.

This displacement usually means moving from rural villages to large cities. This mobilization breaks down all cultural references, social links and natural forms of behaviour that different families have to develop in order to maintain their daily living and survival, exposing them to very complex adaptation dynamics that are generally accompanied by deep poverty. The passage from the rural to the urban environment is made at a very high cost to group and individual psychic dynamics that threaten or paralyze their capacity for self-regulation.

We will go into this later, when we describe an example of a Sandwork process.

Let us first make just one theoretical observation about Sandwork inside our Jungian framework.

As Jungian psychologists, is there something we can do about this reality?

The contributions that psychology has introduced in the course of the last hundred years have had a great impact in enriching our capacity to see reality and helping us make visible what remains invisible around us.

This has allowed our psyche to "incorporate" our experiences from the individual unconscious and from the collective unconscious.

We could also say that, thanks to this evolution that has "affected" our individual consciousness, little by little in these latter times, another field of experiences has started to emerge: the collective consciousness.

By collective consciousness we are referring to the experience of knowing – from an individual consciousness – that we form part of a collective that affects us and which we affect with each one of our actions. We are an individual consciousness that forms part of a system. Or as C.G. Jung wrote: "Hardly the little finger knows itself as member of the hand".

Unfortunately, this collective consciousness has developed more from the destructive power that we human beings possess than from our potential to establish bridges and build from our Eros.

We could say that Expressive Sandwork is an expression of the activation of this collective consciousness that begins in a human being's "loving" field.

The possibility of putting Expressive Sandwork into practice would not have been possible if the need to intervene in a social context had not taken place first in the individual consciousness. During the different processes of choosing the volunteers to participate in the Expressive Sandwork projects, we systematically asked what their motives to approach this project were, and the answer we received over and over was the following:

"I want to participate because I feel isolated while working in my private practice".

What is Expressive Sandwork?

Expressive Sandwork is based on three structures: firstly, the symbolic function, secondly the bond between the child and the facilitator, which develops during the process and can regain the primary relationship, and thirdly the group, which holds the (child-adult) dyads together like an alchemical vessel.

Before continuing with our presentation, we would like to share with you our difficulty in transmitting one of the most important aspects of our work: the emotional atmosphere that is created during this process.

It is one of the transforming forces of Expressive Sandwork, affecting both the children and the volunteers equally.

Physical and Dynamic Setting

In a large room, twelve children are immersed in silent concentration, each one sitting or standing in front of a sand tray, busy creating their own inner worlds.

On a large table in the middle of the room or on the floor are boxes with countless miniature figures and objects, arranged by category: people, animals, houses, cars, trees, bottle corks, shells and marbles.

Among the boxes, cluttered full of toys and the individual sand trays, which are aligned along the walls, there is a hustle and bustle. Countless times the children move back and forth between the table and their sand trays, carrying a small animal, two building blocks, three marbles, and a handful of toy cars. No child disturbs any other. Each one seems preoccupied with his or her own thoughts.

Beside each sand tray sits an adult. Sometimes their presence is so discreet that they are almost unperceivable. If we look at them carefully, we notice that now and again, their faces unexpectedly blush, revealing that he or she is deeply moved.

If we want to sum up the structure of Expressive Sandwork, we could say that it is a system which contains multiple sub-systems.

We would like to show how a child represents this systemic structure in the sand tray itself. A 14-year-old girl has built this image. For her, Sandwork was about nurturing and caring.

Here we show you the miniatures she used: a doctor, a nurse, a pram and milk bottles.

And here you see the picture.

Here you see nurses and doctors, each one caring for a baby in the pram. In the middle on a round table there are baby bottles, nicely prepared. The numbers of the pairs (nurse and baby) correspond exactly to the number of children and adults in this project.

Besides the symbolic expressions of this representation (the mandala-like shape in the centre) it is also a realistic description of the group dynamic: there is a profound trust that all individuals have their place, they are cared for and respected.

Throughout the sessions a "psychic space" will be created between them, which in a way isolates them from their surroundings. Little by little, emotional bridges are built between this child and his or her facilitator, and at the same time, on another level, among each of those participating in the experience.

The work is carried out over at least 12 sessions of one hour each.

Each session takes place on the same tray, together with the same facilitator who the child chooses in the first session. This constancy in the elements – the space, the tray and the facilitator – is essential to favour the atmosphere of trust throughout the process. During the process, little by little, the ability to play awakens and the psyche's symbolic function manifests through the construction of the different images.

For all this to take place, as well as the empathy and an amount of "psychic sensitivity", we need one of our most primitive instincts to be activated: the drive to activity.

Together with this observable part of the process, there is often a more intimate and – many times – invisible process: the building of the bond between the volunteer and the child.

The dynamic that is established, reminds us – step by step and session by session –, of the primary relationship of the child with his or her parent figures.

These bridges become new references. Deep and lasting bonds different to those they have had up till then.

They are emotional bridges that enrich the inter-subjective experience so necessary for the development of the psyche; yet at the same time, act as intra-psychic bridges that allow the activation of the auto-regulating process so necessary to balance a psyche subject to situations that often overwhelm the possibilities of being assimilated.

Beside the bond between child and facilitator, other inter-subjective experiences are activated and developed among all those participating in the process. In this way, children, volunteers and instructors become resonators and activators of an ancestral memory that reminds us that we belong to a wholeness in which we participate through invisible bonds.

The joy and the nature of the connection that, week by week, can be perceived in the encounter of all the participants in this process – the volunteers and those being "accompanied" – give it a ritualistic connotation. Perhaps the strength of this connection is derived precisely from our need to recover and activate these spaces of bonding with the Other.

The following is a description by a school teacher whose role was to assist the whole group in a Sandwork project as an observer.

> "I will just be an observer. The volunteers have to contain the children," I thought to myself. But it wasn't like that and I'm happy it wasn't. I was there entirely, physically, intellectually, emotionally. I was looking with my eyes and with my heart at the volunteer-child duo and I was invaded with emotions that I could differentiate this time. I grew alongside these couples. Most of them looked alike. A few nights in a row I dreamed about digging in the sand.
>
> At one point, in the middle of the project, I was tired and felt cold. The atmosphere was heavy. I feel pain in my arms and shoulders. I feel burdened. I hear a child patting down the sand. The noise rumbles in my ears. It's the only sound I can hear. I feel pain in my whole body. Maybe these children felt similar pains. I look at the volunteers' faces and I see their pain also. We all share this pain. At the end of the session, the child who was patting down the sand looks at me. His face is peaceful, he seems to have left all his pain in the sand and I understood that".

Building the Expressive Sandwork "Systems"

The Children

The choice of the children who will participate in the Expressive sandwork process is carried out by the leaders of the vulnerable communities which we approach.

We have tried to avoid establishing any criteria for the selection of the children. For us, any child who wants to "play with the sand" can be part of the project. But, although there is not a real selection process, we have found that they have been chosen following the intuition and common sense of the community leaders.

Among those children we have found – after evaluating their profiles – that we can identify at least four patterns:

- a chaotic pattern; a depressive one; an anxiety pattern; and
- children with an expected behaviour pattern for their age.

This heterogeneity in which we find strong and healthy children working next to problematic ones has a powerful effect in the group. Using a physics metaphor we can say that by resonance, the vibration of the different individuals who form the group (children and adults), tends to find a "group vibration" which moves towards harmony. Maybe because of this and due to the fact that in every session each child has "its own adult" just for itself, it is very easy for the children to follow and respect the few rules that are given: work on your own; work in silence and, if you need to, speak only with your adult; do not disturb the others; and don't throw the sand out of the box.

The Volunteers

As for the volunteers, there is a precise and strict selection process that takes place at the beginning of each project. The prospective volunteers come from different professions: they could be teachers, social workers, retired people, artists, students … "even" psychologists and psychotherapists are welcome!

The most important criteria in the selection process is their ability to contain their emotions, and to be reliable. They have to guarantee their presence at every session and meeting, without exception, throughout the process, as they cannot be substituted.

The volunteers receive a short but intensive training.

Two sessions of self experience in sandwork are an essential part of this training.

It is obvious that the unconscious of each child activates an intense emotional response in the facilitators' psyche. That's why the volunteers are assisted by the project leaders during the whole project.

There are several group meetings where the volunteers can share the experience of the sessions, the emotional impact, the doubts, fears and preoccupations.

The alchemical reaction between the volunteer and the child begins from the first minutes in which the volunteer encounters the child they happen to work with. We don't assign a child to an adult or vice versa. In the first session, the child "chooses" the adult with whom he or she is going to work with throughout the entire process.

The adults are already in the room, sitting beside the sandtrays, and then, at a certain point, the children enter all together. They have been told: "Just choose a sandtray". But of course in a couple of minutes time, they have also "chosen" the adult, who was sitting next to the sandtray.

For us, this choosing process is based in the "tele" function – described by Levy-Moreno – which we trust as the guide to the bonding process between the child and the person who will be their facilitator, a process that acts both ways.

We are no longer surprised by the synchronicity present in the dynamics between child and facilitator: from possible physical similarities, up to a "coagulation" of elements that existed in the unconscious field and which started to become conscious as the accompanying process unfolded.

The Parents

In all Sandwork projects we try to get the parents involved.

The attitude of the volunteers with the parents is obviously similar to their attitude with the child in a Sandwork session: listening attentively without giving any advice; giving value to their perceptions and giving importance to their role as parents.

The parents, in a non-verbal way, perceive a new quality, which they themselves might not have experienced before. Often they notice the changes in the children during and after the Sandwork project and they ask insistently if siblings could also participate next time.

The parents are never allowed to attend the sessions and will never see a Sandwork construction. The task of some volunteers is to protect the session hermetically from outside curiosity. It is a difficult task, like keeping the alchemical vessel intact, because Sandwork has a tremendous fascination.

Presentation of two Examples

To continue, we would like to present two cases that will show you the context within which we are using Expressive Sandwork.

First Example

The first example of the Expressive Sandwork process is a 12-year-old boy, member of a displaced family from the Amazonas area.

The family consists of the father, the mother, the child, his twin brother (who also participated in our programme), an 11-year-old sister and another 3-year-old brother.

They had to run away from their hometown because guerrillas threatened the father directly – he was a successful shop-owner – and they had to undertake a very risky boat trip on the river that lasted 22 days. During this journey they had to travel through a region where the violence involving the Colombian armed conflict was very intense.

After their arrival in Bogotá they moved into a small house, sub-divided into numerous rooms but equally small, rented out to different families, located a few blocks from Bogota's area called The Bronx, which is one of the most dangerous areas of Bogotá. It is inhabited by more or less 2000 indigents or homeless, the so called "people of the streets". There you can find the stuff of your worst shadow fantasies: any kind of drug, guns, pornography, sex ... also a hit man at a very low cost. All these things have given The Bronx a well-deserved reputation of being the "deepest realm of Hell".

From the first day, the boy's behaviour showed him to be a well educated, happy, formal and friendly child He was very attentive and careful in each of his constructions.

Along the different trays of his process we can recognize the need to work on his transition from his hometown to the capital city's urban environment, as well as his adaptation to the latter.

Right from the beginning, his facilitator observed, as a significant element, the alternating presence of rural and urban environments.

We will present here several of his Sandwork trays in chronological order. All the titles correspond to how the child called each of the scenes he created:

"A Castle in the Woods"

The first sand tray represents a solid building – which the child later acknowledges as a castle – in the middle of a rural or jungle-like environment.

During the construction of this scene the volunteer was very surprised by the way his child worked. Brick by brick and with a lot of patience he built a solid structure in the middle of the sand tray. And after this, he continued creating little scenes around it: a pond filled with fishes and ducks; a house on top of which he put hens and chickens barraged by a cat on the roof, and so on. This construction touched his volunteer emotionally and deeply, he was surprised by the emergence of these feelings out of the blue. After this contact he started to get used to this experience. Almost along the entire process, each session moved him emotionally.

"Foremen Constructing Buildings"

In the next session, the construction with an urban setting catches one's attention, without any natural elements such as trees or animals, with many foremen and construction machines. There is a type of road almost encircling it, and suggesting a one-way movement.

The volunteer felt uncomfortable with this image that contrasted clearly with the previous sand tray.

"The Importance of Nature"

Here we can find a mixture of rural and urban elements, which could suggest a progressive adaptation to the city. There are several elements of the environment in which the boy lived: the river full of fishes; lots of trees placed very near to each other. In the middle, we can see a bridge that connects the river with a wall that he said was part of a town.

In this sand tray, figures that the child identified as female workers appear. These elements could represent his working mother, who has had to take on the role of the provider for the family, as the father had not found any way to provide. The figure of a soldier placed at the wall, of whom the child didn't say anything, caught our attention

"School with Traffic and the Sea"

In this sand tray he built brick by brick a wall surrounding an inner structure that he identified as a school. Outside the wall, co-exist two different environments, represented by the sea and the traffic.

A little further on in his process, he presented a sand tray which he called "The City of Bogotá" which apparently represents – in a very detailed way – the gradual and progressive "adjustment process" to living in the city.

This first city becomes more complex in a new sand tray which he called: *"A City that becomes Another City"*

What is noticeable in this tray is the process of building an extremely elaborate bridge, full of detailed work.

After this sand tray, he built another that he called: *"A Country with Houses and Animals and a Sea"* where apparently he has managed to integrate within the same network – a country – the different external and internal geographies that had been disassociated.

In the next tray, something unexpected was built: an armed conflict which he called: *"When the War of Independence Began"*

This scene shocked the volunteer who didn't expected it after the previous sand trays. For the boy, it was the brutal emerging of the situation that finally forced him and his family to leave their home.

What is noticeable is the detours the child had to take through all the previous sand trays in order to be able to approach this construction which is a clear allusion to the armed conflict that affected his life so deeply.

We could say that the psyche sought a ring-road in order to "see" and confront this painful reality.

We cannot but be amazed at how this process is harmonized by a figure in the middle sitting in a lotus position, which is a contrast to the rest of the soldiers confronting each other.

The facilitator's perception was that at the end of the process the child developed strong inner skills.

Second Example

The second example we would like to present is of a six-year-old girl, whose work with sand not only helped her come to terms with a great burden, but it also had a positive effect on the families in her neighbourhood, because it allowed them to discover a new level of solidarity.

From the first session, the facilitator became aware that the little girl demonstrated that she was under great psychological pressure. She piled on an enormous quantity of objects into her sand tray, especially kitchenware and food, mixed in with insects, serpents, soldiers and small children. She filled up one of the pans with sand and pretended to be cooking. Suddenly, she knocked everything over, stirred them all, furious, she threw everything out and even broke some of the objects. At the end of the session, she covered parts of the tray with a piece of cloth.

In the middle of the chaos, the facilitator was especially impressed with a scene in which a reptile, with wide open jaws, approaches a baby in a pram. She wrote in her notes: "When I lifted the cloth from the right-hand bottom side and I saw the reptile and the fallen cow again, I started to tremble, I felt very cold … I was shocked, my whole body was shaking… I have a sense of something bouncing back… it overwhelms me…"

This emotional reaction and several other scenes in later sessions suggested severe problems in the child and the hypothesis of on-going violence or sexual abuse.

As the facilitators were not psychotherapists, and from an institutional point of view, they were not authorized to suggest this possibility without filing a complaint with the police, the subject was left unresolved for the time being. Expressive Sandwork would continue over a couple of months and the project included several meetings with the parents.

The little girl's representations became less and less chaotic. It seemed especially important to the child to distinguish clearly between good and evil. In the tenth session, these areas were well defined: the girl erected a high barrier in the sand and moved across to the facilitator's side—where the good area was located— as if she were sharing it with the adult volunteer, in order to be as separate as possible from the evil area.

In this session the facilitator perceived the child's strong sense of intimacy, as well as her search for trust.

In the next session something similar takes place: once again the facilitator perceives a sense of closeness and intimacy, while the same barrier creates a separation with the outside world. The girl played at the volunteer's side.

The day after this session the little girl asked to talk to her teacher, and said she had something important to tell her. The teacher agreed to listen and the little girl told her she was being sexually abused by one of her neighbours.

The teacher immediately began the medical, psychological and legal procedures for these cases. The school doctor and school psychologist, as well as the police, contacted the little girl's parents.

The accused, the father of a fourteen-year-old girl who was also participating in the project, left the neighbourhood a few hours later.

The fear of the children from the entire apartment block had been removed.

The parents of other children were very alarmed but they reacted without panicking, and over the following days, they began to talk with their daughters. Two other girls reported similar incidents that involved the same man.

In less favourable conditions, when a common enemy in a poverty-stricken and crime-ridden environment is identified, this type of revelation can easily unleash a reaction of hate and even more violence. However, in this case the Sandwork project had promoted solidarity among the affected families, especially among the women, and this united them.

The problem was solved by socially binding the resources available within the very same community.

As the children were protected, the mothers were able to face the reality in a serene and rational way. This was particularly evident in the solidarity shown towards the wife and daughter of the abuser, who were terrified that they might suffer some kind of revenge. On the other hand, it was a tacit law within the Bronx that the men would not wait for the police to find the abuser.

As to the little girl whose therapy with the Sandwork had initiated the episode, the sessions as well as her growing confidence in the facilitator had strengthened her own self-esteem and had given her the security that she would be listened to.

It must be pointed out that she had not gone to her facilitator, nor had she requested some form of intervention, which would not have been possible in a direct way. She preserved her facilitator's role, and sought help in the most adequate place, basically her school, and a social institution. She was incredibly efficient, probably because the necessary structure had already begun to emerge in her. Although the school and the teachers existed prior to her Sandwork experience, it was only this kind of specific work that offered her enough inner strength and self-esteem which enabled her to resort to approaching the external resources that had already been in place for her, in order to use them adequately.

After two years, this child – who is now ten years old – could participate again in a sandwork project.

It is obvious that the sandwork projects need continuity in the same community. This happens in many situations because the volunteers are willing to continue. Also, the organizations with whom we collaborate are always trying to build long-term interventions.

In Colombia we have collaborated with the following organizations:

- "Community of San Egidio" a lay charity organization based in Italy, known worldwide.

- Parroquia del Voto Nacional of Padre Darío Echeverri (a Catholic Priest, known internationally as peace mediator in the armed conflict in Colombia).

- "Batuta" a Colombian organization initiative that has representatives throughout the entire country and promotes music and forms orchestras. We had made an alliance with this organization which provides places for conducting sandwork projects and facilitates the connection between our volunteers and the children of the communities where they work. With them we have carried out different processes in Bogotá, Medellín and Barranquilla.

- "Suramericana" a huge investment group that promotes social responsibility among their workers. They have given us financial support in our projects in Bogotá, Medellín and Barranquilla.

Results

Up to this moment, we have carried out ten Sandwork processes in different cities of Colombia.

Between 2011 and 2013, we carried out a test created by our team to identify trauma in the children we work with

The most significant changes we came across were:

- A decrease in the levels of anxiety and aggression.

- A better relationship with themselves: self-image, confidence, creativity and persistence.

- A better relationship with others: communication, empathy, expression of his/her emotions.

- Improvements in his/her cognitive processes: attention, concentration, motivation, capacity to learn.

During the sessions they always achieved an attitude of calmness and confidence independently of their initial behavior.

Testimonies

Nearing the end of our lecture, we want to give a voice directly to the children and to the volunteers who participated in the different Sandwork projects that we had led:

Volunteers:

* I feel that we have participated in a process that transcends realities. We are no longer the same as before.
* After the sandwork process I encountered problems that I was able to deal with better than before, because I could assist myself just like I assisted the child during sandwork.
* For the first time I feel a part of a worldwide planted field.
* Many times I wondered: "Who has been helped by whom?"
* The group as a container was fundamental in all the aspects that are perceivable only from within. It is a group energy that cannot be expressed in words.

Children:

* During this project I could open up, unburden myself, even if I didn't speak…. it mattered very much to me that somebody cared about me, even if she didn't say so.
* This project calmed me, I'm not as hasty and rash as before. …
* I won't forget this project and when I grow up I will volunteer somewhere too.

Some of the testimonials and descriptions have been reported by sandwork volunteers from Rumania. We thank the Rumanian colleagues for their generous contribution.

A Policy of Dialogue

Vito Marino De Marinis

(Italy, CIPA)

A Tale of Three Associations

My brief considerations describe a shift in the relationships among the three Italian Jungian psychoanalytic associations, which decided to overcome a dimension of competition, conflict, suspicion or indifference. The AIPA society, whose full name is Associazione italiana psicologia analitica, was founded in Rome in 1962. CIPA stands for Centro italiano psicologia analitica and it came to life four years later, in 1966. ARPA is the acronym for Associazione per la ricerca psicologica applicata, and was established in 1987. AIPA, CIPA and ARPA have begun a process of dialogue and reciprocal knowledge.

However, as we know, dialogue, can be unsettling. Brotherhood and solidarity, necessary to true encounter, arise together with their shadow: the vision of the other as a rival.

The old *homo homini lupus* rises from its ashes and, as the spirit of Mercury, creates misunderstandings, fear and suspicion. However, if we are anchored in the values of the Jungian world, awareness of evil does not exempt us from pursuing what we think to be the good. In this respect the following thoughts attempt to describe the deep meaning of choice, its urgency or necessity in the sense meant by the ancient Greeks.

One starting point has been written in this paper by Gianni Nagliero: "I would like to talk about a … dream in quotation marks … that the various schools of different analytic associations, rather than being confined within strict barriers, would open themselves to other analytic associations" (Nagliero 2008, p. 33).

That dream has started to become a true and complex experience, from which arise my following remarks.

The Good Policy

This experience clearly belongs to the realm of politics, which is the management or government for the common good, based on structured and conscious purposes. A policy implies, first of all, a choice – a choice of a specific direction.

Today the word politics, at least in Italy, has become highly negative. It brings with it an aura of personal interest and corruption. Therefore, we want to go back to the classical meaning of politics, given in Aristotle's Ethics: politics is about searching for the common good. Aristotle's moral value is in clear opposition to the borrowed Machiavellianism prevailing today, in which the ethical dimension is often lost not only in the means but also in the ends.

Policy, therefore, is first a choice and then an action, action that tries to transform the existing state of affairs. The action, in this case, is aimed at creating a real dialogue among Jungian analytic associations with the goal to achieve, in the end, a new entity, a confederation of associations. My concern, however, is not about quantitative increase, which would allow us to be more and more influential in relation to the community. What I do care about is the moral value that is required to achieve the goal, which implies the idea of dialogue, solidarity and community. The whole exercise will bring our associations closer to the idea of the world in which we would like to live.

Jungian Associations: Community versus Proselytism

However, the Jungian associations have a history, a past that affects us and of which we need to become conscious.

According to Zipparri (2013), the Jung Institute of Zurich can be considered the first Jungian analytic association. Its main feature was not the formation of new analysts, but the keeping of a community, a club of analyzed people who got together again "to support each other in their psychological and spiritual development". In this context, the idea of community was predominant and it had a great value for the ethical quality of the group.

In the subsequent decades, the analytic associations have evolved as training venues and have sunk into the quantitative dimension of proselytizing. They have become increasingly large and influential "in promoting the study and development of Jungian thought", to use a frequent recite in the statutes of various associations.

The aim of becoming bigger and bigger, and more influential than ever, often has prevailed at the expense of the other goal, *id est*, to build a community that helps and supports the development and maturation of the individual.

The dominance of the quantitative growth obsession has often resulted in suffering of individuals who have attempted to find "community" in smaller groups, sometimes of an endogamous nature, if not overtly incestuous. These contradictions, along with other reasons, have facilitated the processes of splitting. In fact today, in Italy there are four Jungian analytic associations among whom, as expected, negative projections frequently predominate. CIPA was born out of a split in AIPA, ARPA was born from a split in CIPA and so on.

Sociology tells us that, for the policy of large numbers, this result is inevitable, almost "natural". I believe, however, that it is not necessary to subdue our minds and actions to such "naturalness". We should not accept passively the destruction of humanity that is produced whenever schisms or estrangements occur in groups.

Identity and Competition

Sure we can continue to compete, on the grounds of personal interests, about who is more Jungian or post-Jungian. And we can meet each other with fear or contempt. Or we may close ourselves in the search for illusions or prejudices about the purity of our particular symbolic universe. And we can also cultivate, in small groups, eso-teric cultures and take simple theoretical hypotheses or "provisional beliefs", as Jung called them (Jung, 1935, p. 3-20), as absolute truths,

In cultivating these mistakes we are not only participating, but becoming prisoners of the spirit of the time. The Western world is based on the false belief that competition will eventually bring wellbeing to all, even to the losers. However, by following such a belief, you build a world that: "is inhospitable to human solidarity and trust and friendly cooperation". It is a culture that encourages us to feel "surrounded by rivals, competitors in the infinite game of always doing better than others" (Bauman, 2013, p.51).

All this would lead to entrenching ourselves in the narrow boundaries of our schools and associations, thereby stiffening and impoverishing our thinking. This is a negative solution. It is opposed to the basic ethics of our profession that is founded on solidarity and dialogue, as we shall see in the next few paragraphs.

Security in a Frightened Environment

Without a doubt, today we live in a frightened global community which, instead of opening itself, leads, motivated by fear, to a collapse and closing off. The cages enclose us in petty parochialisms, in rigid groups holding on to partial discoveries portrayed as absolute truths. In fact, the era in which we live has seen a crisis of the great truths and is exposed to neoliberal globalization in the economic field. The culture of our era is a scared culture, a culture of fear, frightened and even threatened by other cultures which are getting closer and closer each day. In this situation, individuals seem to organize themselves around the need for security, their principal aim being to protect themselves from fear.

Security is becoming the key issue in a world that has lost its certainties. In fact, the definitions attached to our age are "the era of uncertainty" or "the liquid society". In our era, it seems that the contraction, caused by fear, produces the resurgence of racism and narrow-minded parochialism on the social level.

We see the reflections of this "era of uncertainty" in our professional environment: the anguish drives us to close ourselves, in an egomaniacal way, in our private sphere. We shut ourselves into small groups that close themselves off by relying on theories taken for absolute truths and rejecting all types of otherness. Or we wander around in the presence of a manic state that eschews the slow times and the silence of reflection which are needed for any inner evolution.

We are looking for certainties and become prey to the returning scientism. Even in our professional environment, the logic of quantity, son of the economic culture, seems to subdue all other values.

Bad Times call for Resistance

Facing such an invasion, I think the first and foremost thing to do is to constitute pockets of resistance for an ethical world, which is in conflict with the spirit of the time. We should consider solidarity, as one of the foundations of our common experience. It is a primary value, and one of the possible answers to the widespread perception of crisis – a crisis escaping enduring resolutions, which seems to be a metaphor of the post-modern human condition**.)**. This is a condition characterized by a perverse relationship with time. It is the inability to think about the future. Ours is, according to Levinas, a "time without promises" (Levinas, 1982).

Transcendence has abandoned the man and the world. The future becomes agonizingly uncertain: we live in the time of uncertainty. This uncertainty makes us frightened and helpless. But if fear does not predominate in our minds, if the sense of helplessness does not slip into bitterness, we can accept the crisis as an opportunity, an opportunity for openness to new possibilities, to change.

We already know that action is without warranty, and this is reflected in our theoretical conviction and all the more in our analytic work. The state of uncertainty and action without guarantees can produce anxiety and disorientation in the mind, but I think they could also clear the mind in meeting the other in their own individuality, thereby facilitating a general greater freedom to think, learn, live and change.

We become at the same time more vulnerable but also better directed toward an individual encounter with reality, which is our only possibility and responsibility. Exactly because the myth of infinite and irreversible progress is gone, the human condition should be treated as an uncertain and unpredictable adventure.

It is sufficient to think of the last period as one in which the one-dimensional economical approach – bearing efficiency as its only value – did not deliver what it had promised, i.e. greater happiness and security. Furthermore, it has revealed itself to be an illusion: it has not brought security, but has corroded the ethical dimension.

It is necessary, in this context, not to stop being sensible and to retain the capacity for outrage, remembering that the sphere of ethics is the basis of our work and, therefore, feel called to assume greater responsibility.

The Foundations of our Profession

At the base of our profession, there is in fact respect for the other and for his/her otherness, and there is compassion for their suffering. Only respect and compassion can open us to dialogue. Aurigemma extracts from Jung this definition of a good therapist: "an individual morally and intellectually well-structured, driven in their activities primarily from a deep feeling of human solidarity" (Aurigemma, 2008, p. 7).

If the myth of certain and inevitable progress has collapsed, and the future becomes uncertain, we nevertheless cannot give in to the mistrust and bitterness of the present times. And if we let go of the psychic contraction produced by fear, we can bet on the future (Morin, 2002). In such a future, an ethical dimension, specific to our world and closely linked to the idea of solidarity, can be achieved. The future, in this respect, is not only the deterministic result of the present, but it is also a bet, linked to the goals to be achieved. The future can also be made, it can be built.

Promise and Desire

The bridge to the future can in fact be thrown from two pillars: promise and desire.

The promise looks like the (implicit) one we make to our patients: to be reliable, that we will not die, and will not go crazy in the months or years required for the analytic therapy. On this promise is based the possibility of trust that may be enabled by the other. Promises are also important in the encounters with others in general and specifically among associations. To others we promise that competition will not transcend the dimension of solidarity and respect.

We are the agents of desire, in the specific form of creating a real and continuous dialogue among Jungian associations. The desire can produce those actions which ensure that the basic values of our profession find accomplishment. Desire is both commitment and challenge. It is an uncertain and complex adventure, not a secure and predictable route. The "trail of desire" is traced by walking, by anyone who observes his movement in the world and the movement of the world itself.

The movement is needed to continue to punctuate the dialogue, despite tumbles and misunderstandings, to continue to think, to keep us psychically alive.

Of course, we can meet each other narcissistically, expecting only mirroring and so, easily slip into contempt for the other ... Or we can, out of fear, entrench ourselves in stuffy groups. But we can bet on a good feeling, on a strong attitude, friendship perhaps.

Friendship among Associations

Here we come to friendship among associations. Maybe it's a stretch of a linguistic term that nowadays describes a fact that occurs between individuals, in the intimacy of face-to-face. But the concept of friendship can be extended to allow other meanings that enhance its value.

In fact, Hannah Arendt proposes a different and wider meaning of friendship. Friendship is not private but public, and therefore political. It refers to the Aristotelian concept of philia: "the friendship between citizens, is one of the fundamental conditions for the welfare of the city" (Arendt, 2006, p.84)

For ancient Greeks, the essence of friendship consisted in conversation. For Arendt (2006), the world is not human because human beings inhabit it. Only through the dialogue between people the world becomes human: "We humanize what is happening in the world and in ourselves only by speaking, and in this talk, we learn to become human".

The ancient Greeks called this humanity, philanthropy. It is realized through the dialogue of friendship, as it is manifested in the willingness to share the world with other people.

A Little Respect

If we look closely at the meaning of the term dialogue we can, in my view, grasp the possibility that is inherent in respect.

The main component of friendship is respect. Friendship is not exploitation or manipulation or complicity against a third party. Friendship is based on trust and respect for each other, in each other's own uniqueness.

According to De Monticelli (2003, p. 217), respect is: "the feeling of the value of the other as such by virtue of its uniqueness and (beyond) the detection of any of its property."

Respect structures itself by freeing the mind from any complex. It is deeply fair-minded, and therefore it is the basis of the process of understanding the other.

Respect is a virtue that arises from the possibility to govern our passions. To open towards the other, in this case towards other associations, which can mean, first of all, to become vulnerable, forthcoming. We should be prepared to accept risks in approaching the other, in feeling their proximity which is necessary for any real dialogue.

What can a Jungian Association do?

This is not easy. A dialogue can be disturbing. But engagement in dialogue can be rewarding. Natoli (2002) observes: "recent events, but also general history, are there to show that where societies lack virtues, they tend in the long run to break apart and break down (…) or are reduced to a condition unpleasant to live in".

Our small societies, our associations, can deteriorate into a condition unpleasant to live in … All of us have experienced such a situation. However, due to the particular nature of our work, our associations have an essential value. They may or may not facilitate our capacity for inner growth and our ability to be effective analysts.

One of the elements on which we base our confidence in what we think or act, is the sense of belonging to the community of the competent. This belonging is a complex bond, divided between the cognitive and the emotional dimensions. This bond necessarily affects our basic trust when we are in the consulting room.

For example, it is not so simple and obvious to maintain the confidence that what we do today may produce, in three or ten years, growth and development. What we do today lives along with other facts that occurred yesterday, that perhaps we understood only partially, and will be shaped by still other events that will occur in the coming sessions. This confidence can be supported, at least partially, by the idea of the existence of the group of our colleagues who have shared, over a period of time, our own confidence in the therapeutic process.

Risks and Opportunities

As I tried to show, the journey that our organizations have embarked on is not easy. It is, however, necessary. The elements that can create problems, the complexes of each individual and also the past complexes, are always present. But, as we know, every human situation carries within the sense of risk and the possibility for a solution. It is our duty to manage them, or, at least, to try to manage.

The desire for a friendship to blossom requires commitment and undertaking an uncertain and unpredictable path. Only this way, however, can we practice solidarity. Solidarity that goes with formal membership as defined in the "politically correct" dictionary does not interest us. But it has great value when it becomes an action, a commitment, a shared effort.

Starting from these actions of "incarnated dialogue", the idea of community becomes a concrete experience and a way of life. By this way we become neighbors, living next to each other.

The proximity, in fact, is approaching another not to subjugate him or her to our needs, not to create a narcissistically oriented mirror, but to activate the emotional dimension that determines a recognition of them as a similar being, a travelling companion in the adventure of life.

In our specific case, the adventure began more than a hundred years ago with the birth of analytic psychology. It's an adventure that unfolds from generation to generation of analysts, and in which each of us needs to live with both enthusiasm and responsibility.

Bibliography

Arendt, H. (2006). *L'umanità in tempi bui*. Milano: Raffaello Cortina. Published in English as *On Humanity in Dark Times. Thoughts about Lessing*.
Aurigemma, L. (2008). *Il risveglio della coscienza*. Torino: Bollati Boringhieri
Bauman, Z. (2013). *"La ricchezza di pochi avvantaggia tutti". Falso!* Bari: Laterza. To be published in English as *Does the Richness of the Few Benefit Us All?*.
De Monticelli, R. (2003). *L'ordine del cuore*. Milano: Garzanti.
Jung, C.G.(1935).Principles of practical psychotherapy. Collected Works Vol.16. London: Routledge & Kegan, London 1954.
Levinas E.(1982), *Etica e infinito*. Castelvecchi ed., Roma, 2012.
Morin, E. (2002). *Il metodo 5. L'identità umana*. Milano: Raffaello Cortina.
Nagliero G., Grosso W.(2008), *Analisi in età evolutiva*, Vivarium ed., Milano
Zipparri, I. (2013), paper presented at a CIPA conference in Rome, March 2013.

From Splitting to Collaboration: Repairing the Conflict Among Associations

Gianni Nagliero

(Italy, AIPA)

Introduction

The purpose of this presentation is to share with our colleagues our own passionate experience of a new kind of collaboration that has been created among different psychoanalytic associations in Italy, in the hope of a fruitful exchange through the views, comments, criticisms and suggestions offered.

We represent two Italian associations, AIPA which was founded in 1961, and CIPA which was founded in 1966, after a group of colleagues split from AIPA. We are pleased to say that, shortly after our proposal for a presentation at this congress, even ARPA, the third Italian Jungian association, born in 1987 after a split from CIPA, has begun to participate in this collaborative experience. This commitment to facilitate future collaboration on the part of our colleagues from ARPA, guided by their President, Ferruccio Vigna, is very important and promises well for the future of Analytical Psychology in Italy.

This new spirit of collaboration led to the joint conference held by AIPA and CIPA in 2011 to mark the occasion of the 50th anniversary of the death of Jung and of the founding of AIPA. Again in 2012, the three associations organized a conference in Turin to commemorate two important and significant figures in the Jungian landscape, James Hillman and Mario Trevi.[1] Finally, every event organized by one of our associations is advertised to the other two and all members are invited to participate.

However, what I wish to discuss here is not so much our common celebration of events. Instead, what we would like to be able to achieve, is to try to understand what can be the basis for a joint work among associations, taking into account the theoretical and clinical differences that affect us all as Jungians.

---

1 Vito Marino De Marinis, Gianni Nagliero e Ferruccio Vigna (Editors), "Maestri a confornto", Moretti e Vitali, Bergamo (Italy) (2013)

Why so many Divisions?

From its origins, Jungian theory has been characterized by its richness of innovative ideas. My reflection, therefore, follows from the fact that the thought at the basis of our Jungian identity, is a very broad one indeed, addressing many different aspects of the human endeavor, not only the psycho-therapeutic method of analysis. This vastness of Jungian reflections urges a similar breadth of meditation on the part of all of us.

We obviously consider that Jung's far-reaching reflections are a great legacy he has left to us but a similar legacy necessarily requires further development and this can lead us to take different paths and to arrive at conclusions that may not be shared by us all.

In the Jungian environment, in my opinion, disagreement seems to have been more frequent than in other psychoanalytically oriented schools. The disagreement among us Jungian has all too often led to divisions within the family. In the case of CIPA, ARPA and AIPA, but also in the recent spin-off of some AIPA colleagues, there was no project of founding another school or another association with a different theory. We all worked within the context of Jungian thought and were all part of the great Jungian family, the IAAP.

In my opinion, the main reason for these kinds of splits can be traced to the interrelationship between the vastness of Jungian thought and Jung's tendency to act towards his pupils as a permissive and encouraging father, rather than as a strong and uncompromising one.

The Magnitude of Jungian Thought

I believe that Jung was aware of the complexity and unresolved issues of his theory, so much so that he often invited his students and colleagues not to stop there, not to barricade themselves behind his theories, but to try to always go further and find new ways. I've often wondered about the meaning of his famous sentence: "Thank God I'm Jung and not a Jungian." In my opinion, "a Jungian" in this sentence was intended to refer to a fixed, definite, final, immutable attitude towards his theory. Jung and we, Jungian disciples, know very well how any thought which is both complex and in nascent state such as psychoanalytic thinking, is a thought that remains alive only if it can be the object of critical reflection, continuous research and change.

Today I consider this famous phrase of Jung as an exhortation not to remain anchored to Jung's thought, and to avoid any defensive closure – an exhortation to go forward, to try to create an open Jungian environment, capable of welcoming the ideas of others, with a critical and reflexive attitude.

Due to its vastness, and the consequently incomplete nature of

Jung's reflections, and his intolerance of all dogmatisms, we Jungians, have always felt authorized to carry forward ideas and ways of working that best fitted the characteristics of our own personal experiences, even when these differed from those of the master.

But, like any young man who takes a different path from his father, we lived these new ways of thinking with the usual ambivalence and guilt. One of the justifications that we have given was that, fundamentally, we all said roughly the same thing. We had theories that, basically, relied on a "common Jungian denominator".

In some earlier periods, after Jung's passing, all this went almost unnoticed. The "young" community of fellow students of Jung found itself in some way lost and without a strong father, a father who believes strongly in the completeness of his theory and imposes it on his followers. Moreover, this happened in the psychoanalytical environment dominated by a powerful and monolithic Freudian "opponent". In such conditions, the Jungian community has been affected by what we might simply call "primary anxieties of disintegration".

Only some time after the death of Jung it became possible to arrive at a full awareness of the diversity of viewpoints, accepting them both as different and legitimate in the Jungian community.

Only in relatively recent times have different strands of interest and clinical settings been formalized within the general Jungian family (Samuels, 1985).

The expression "common Jungian denominator", popular in Italy, was created, I believe, for more than one reason. First of all, it was exactly in order to avoid the ambivalence and the feeling of guilt in the archetypal relationship between *senex* and *puer*. Secondly, in order to escape the above mentioned primary anxiety. It is an expression born to reassure us, all of us, that we do have a father, even if we think different things and especially if we work in different ways. A slogan that has always kept us together and given us a sense of belonging, enabling us to work as a group, as well as in our external relations.

But today I want to propose another explanation. Besides having a protective effect, the idea and the profession of faith in the "common Jungian denominator", also led us to ignore our differences. Exactly those differences that sometimes make our students confused and astonished in front of the opposite statements of their teachers.

I think that, often, many aspects of the differences between us are the outcome of a way of dealing with the phenomena from different observational standpoints. And I also think that some aspects of our theoretical and clinical Jungian thought have very little of a "common denominator". Or rather, I believe that each of us has drawn different conclusions from the "common denominator", which led us to explore lands that are sometimes distant from each other, often claiming, in turn, the Jungian birthright.

We often hear ourselves saying phrases like: "the most significant Jungian technique is active imagination", or: "No. It is the work on dreams ... on images ... on myths", or: "No. It is the attention to the relationship" and so on.

We cannot keep on proposing opposite readings of Jung's thought and, at the same time, pretending, all of us, that these are "genuinely" Jung's thoughts. This divides us, and, in my humble opinion, was feared by Jung himself. I am convinced that we should not feel obliged in our explorations of Jung's thought to remain in the groove traced by him.

The "common Jungian denominator" therefore, in the way that has been used so far, severely limits Jungian development and has no longer any reason to exist. Jung himself is asking us to proceed, reminding us that it is not important to define ourselves as Jungians on the basis of adherence to his original thinking. He rather asks us to cross new frontiers.

If we accept that we have developed different paths, especially in clinical work, then we should reserve the term "Common Jungian denominator" for some other aspects. First of all, for our reference and our debt of gratitude to Jung for his theoretical proposals, and for his vision of the human psyche, the unconscious and the archetypes of the collective unconscious, the process of individuation, and so on. But I think that we should build on his heartfelt invitation not to be slavishly Jungian, not to fossilize every idea, not to grow "isms".

Jung will finally stop tossing and turning in his grave and will be pleased to see that his followers, or at least a good part of them, can feel themselves Jungian without having to be framed in a frozen and parceled Jungian thought, something he would never have wanted. It is exactly thanks to his attitude as an encouraging father that his followers can feel free to call themselves Jungian even if they have different ways of working, to each other and to the teacher. It is this position that can allow us to identify the differences in our theoretical and clinical ideas and talk about them without fear of being accused of heresy.

Therefore, in our cooperation among associations, we do not belittle differences, but rather point them out in order to study them better and better, with passion, looking along new roads that, starting with Jung, explore new territories. We consider this a specific request of Jung.

Differences within Associations

Today, at least in Italy, the existing theoretical and clinical diversities are not what divides the associations. The diversities are not related to membership of an association. They are evident within the same association. Each of our three associations has colleagues who differ significantly in their theories and clinical practice.

This shows that Jung's is not a saturated theory, and that divisions are only in part motivated by different theoretical ideas. Moreover, we do know that splits originate also from personal conflicts and power struggles. We may say that often the theoretical and clinical diversities have been nothing more than a pretext.

Personal conflicts are thus important, but they are not the focus of this presentation. I take this opportunity to remind all of us, that we should never stop acting as analysts. I do not mean to become like the so-called parlor analysts, often mercilessly portrayed in movies and cartoons.

Instead, it is important to continue our analysis and "self-analysis" even the analysis of our behavior in the life of our associations, in order to consider the unconscious determinants of our conduct. This would avoid many unnecessary conflicts, quarrels during meetings, resignations and migrations from one association to another. Often the sole purpose of these negative events is the gratification of our inner demons, mostly of a narcissistic nature.

A Group Phenomenon

Let us now look at the association as a group of individuals.

One of the primary aims of founding an association would seem to be to protect ourselves, our own ideas, and, in particular, the statements of our master.

This is understandable and agreeable: the founder upholds his method and theory. Equally understandable is his desire not to see his method confused with other methods, or worse, misused.

But, as Jung has always taught, we must be attentive to the other side of the coin: protection from the outside has its drawbacks and the associations runs the risk of becoming encapsulated in fear that meeting with different theories may weaken our own. It can, therefore, happen that a society experiences a fossilization, becoming not only protected but definitely closed in on itself. The result is an association which hides behind the indisputable claims of the founder and sees as an attack, every deviating thought. The association then becomes a fortress that serves only to defend against new ideas, for fear that contamination with the ideas of the other may bring about its end. One could say, using an unfortunately common expression, that this attitude runs the risk of producing societies engaged in a kind of "analytic fundamentalism".

An association must not become a stronghold defended by ramparts. It must be protected of course, but also open to debate. At the level of theory, although, of course, not in the analytic setting, it should be able to open up its boundaries. This kind of attitude allows the association to make valid contributions and to be open to the useful ideas of others.

The all-out defense of the original ideas of the master may well be the best means to deplete those very ideas. Jung, in my opinion, knew this very well and feared exactly this possibility. If change conjures up images of danger both in individuals and in groups, the reaction is often defensive behavior, aimed at maintaining the *status quo*, so as not to allow destabilization, confusion, destructive chaos. The association refers to its leader, draws life from him. A common group fantasy is that the group will stay alive only as long the master or his thinking is alive. Therefore, it has a tendency toward homeostasis. This is perhaps one of the reasons why, when it arrives at a certain number of members, an association tends to split and, even worse, to split between "true" and "false" interpreters of the master's theory.

A New Way to Communicate Among Ourselves

The collaboration we propose is not politically correct or overly conciliatory. It is simply open to the encounter with the ideas of others, especially when they are different. Openness towards the other does not mean homogenizing and rendering banal our own ideas.

Our intention, while we work to improve collaboration among organizations, is not to mix many different ideas and come out just with one. Today, it is not about reunifying all societies into a single Italian Jungian association. Rather, our primary purpose is to work constructively together on the differences between us, not to search for similarities at all costs.

Collaborating means to start from the strong theoretical position of each one of us, the one we have constructed over time, that we have worked with, but at the same time accepting the fact that the other has found a different route. Cooperating, therefore, means talking together, like two old friends who debate, maybe argue, but then have a drink together, because everyone respects the path and the beliefs of the other.

And most importantly, each one of us is prepared to renounce his or her claim to the Jungian copyright, while enriching ourselves through the comparison with different theories, and as a result, with different ways of relating in the consulting room.

And this requires a willingness to take on board the other's ideas or, to paraphrase Jung, to get sick of our own illness! It is important to preserve our willingness to become a friend of those who have differ-ent ideas as well as to stay a friend of those who have taken another theoretical and clinical path, feeling that we are all descendants of the same father and are all grateful to him.

For me, the two most important aims of our associations remain the improvement of our theories and the comparison of our clinical experiences. Both are fundamental in order to facilitate our patients on theirs, and also on our own, individuation paths.

Bibliography

Samuels, A. (1985), *Jung and the Post Jungians.* London: Routledge and Kegan Paul

Thursday, 22 August 2013

Introduction

François Martin-Vallas

Master of Ceremonies

(France, SFPA)

Good morning,

In opening this morning's presentations, dedicated to the question of neuroscience in two quite contrasting approaches, I would like first, if I may, to share with you some brief personal observations on this topic.

We all know that Jung did his internship in psychiatry at the Burghölzli Hospital. We also know that Bleuler gave Jung the task of pursuing research into the Word Association Test. It was a time of classifications, and of typologies, and those tests were intended to perfect such typological classifications. But many people engaged in this type of experiment had found that subjects sometimes failed to respond, were late to respond or missed the point. These atypical responses were therefore considered as vacuous, in other words they were experimental data that had to be excluded from analysis.

The very thing that other experimenters left to one side gave Jung, assisted by his cousin, Franz Riklin, the brainwave to study. He demonstrated by a stroke of remarkable intuition that the anomalies detected during the word association tests, were the result of some affect. And, to prove it, he used one of the most sophisticated techniques of his time: the measure of galvanic response. He designed a galvanometer he then had assembled, in order to conduct the measurements that could verify his hypothesis. So it was that Jung became probably one of the earliest neuroscientists, in the true sense of the word, if not actually the first. It was these researches that soon led to his international reputation; he was barely thirty years old

These same researches drew Freud's attention to him, who saw in them a proof of the existence of the unconscious. But Freud's unconscious was not the same as Jung's. For Freud, consciousness had primacy, and the unconscious was merely the result of what had not become integrated with it and had therefore been repressed. In Jung's case, on the other hand, the unconscious had primacy, and repression alone could not account for it. Jung's definition of the unconscious was simple: in his view, all that is not conscious is the unconscious. The unconscious and all that is not conscious are perfectly synonymous in Jung's terms – this is obviously not the case for Freud.

Personally, I find it truly remarkable that a century later, contemporary neuroscientists should have a definition of the unconscious that is strictly identical with his. And there is a further point that to me is remarkable and that is, that Jung was able to have access to the unconscious through his studies of psychic processes, involving cognitive activity as well as affective dynamics, which from the very start allowed him to have a vision of the unconscious that was both dynamic and all-encompassing. However, over a century later, this is still not the case for many neuroscientists, who persist in their view of the unconscious purely in terms of its cognitive functions, and continue to ignore its affective dynamics.

Fortunately, some, like our Australian colleague, Leon Petchkovsky, are re-running Jung's experiments with twenty first century techniques, and I am willing to bet that very soon a host of neuroscientists will become very interested in his results. Could it be that we are witnessing a *renaissance*, one hundred years later?

A second point concerning Jung's contemporary relevance to modern neuro-science, stems from his ideas of the archetype and of synchronicity. Obviously, his definitions in this context can sometimes appear vague or contradictory and at times, bordering on the magical. But to my mind, there is not a shred of doubt that these ideas are worth reworking, as has been done for some time now by the likes of Maxson McDowell, George Hogenson, Jean Knox, Christian Roesler and myself, among those I am able to name.

I think that these two ideas are very close to current notions of auto-organization and of emergence. They are notions that, these days are unavoidable in the field of biological science.

Clearly, there will be some who will tell me that the idea of an archetype differs greatly from the idea of auto-organization, given that in Jung's terms, it predates the existence of the individual, or even that of our species. To this my response is that reeling back a hundred years or thereabouts, when this idea was first conjured in Jung's mind, nobody could imagine something that is able to determine an organizational structure other than as a pre-existing structure of the stated organization. Thanks to the work of physicists on chaos theory and on the nature of complex systems, the idea of auto-organization has very gradually assumed its rightful place in science as a whole, so that it is now a given both in biology and in developmental psychology.

Still others will counter me by stating that the idea of synchronicity differs greatly from the idea of emergence, on the basis that Jung links synchronicity with an a-causal principle, whereas emergent phenomena are all perfectly deterministic. Well, I am bound to say that there exists a peculiarity in causation that is at the root of emergent phenomena: this causation is specifically retrograde. Here is what I mean:

Ever since Newton, causation is a law of physics, which explains what has occurred and predicts what will happen. By all accounts, then, causation has become synonymous with predictability. Yet, the French mathematician, Poincaré, showed at the end of the IX century that purely deterministic systems exist, which are meanwhile unpredictable. And it is only since the early 70s that physicists have begun to grapple with this anomaly through the study of chaotic systems. Now it strikes me that this Jungian notion of a-causality is precisely applicable to events, which occur quite unpredictably without losing anything of their deterministic character. Once again, Jung appears to have been well ahead of his time.

But it is now time for me to give way to this morning's speakers and to wish you a fruitful day at the congress.

Translated from French by Ann Kutek

Jung's Understanding of Schizophrenia – Is it still Relevant in the "Era of the Brain"

Yehuda Abramovitch

(Israel, IIJP)

A few months ago, while working on this presentation, I was asked by a colleague to do a consultation, needed for forensic purposes. I will tell the story in short and later return to insights relevant to this talk.

We had to deliver an expert opinion in the case of a young woman, aged 23 or 24, accused of having murdered her children. The story was terrible and had many echoes in the news. A young woman, from a Bedouin settlement in the south of the country, waited for her husband to leave for work, then killed her three children. The story went even further. It seemed that she first killed her baby child, then the baby's brother who was one or two years old. The eldest child aged two or three escaped, crying that mother was beating him. He was met by good willing neighbors who calmed the child down and took him back to his mother. She killed him soon afterwards.

I was sure I was going to meet a modern Medea, an evil sorceress motivated by who knows what dark motivations, or at least a very disturbed non-human monster. I was surprised to meet a young woman, clean, tidy, good looking, even coquettish. She spoke good Hebrew (not very common with young Bedouin women). She came from a traditional family, went to school and graduated from high school (again, not very common). She hoped to become a nurse, maybe even a doctor. Actually, she had good grades and had she applied, she could have been considered, and had good chances to be accepted at one of our medical schools. But before she could understand it, at the age of 17, forced by her family and traditions, she found herself married to a cousin twenty years her senior. Soon afterwards she was pregnant, and then again and again. Her husband would leave for work early in the morning and return late in the evening. She was surrounded by lots of family members expecting her to behave. Eventually, she discovered that her husband was on the verge of taking a second wife. For years she had a "GENI", a kind of an evil spirit talking to her, saying dirty words and pushing her to commit suicide or alternatively kill her husband or her children. She struggled with this voice but it became more and more present, more difficult to resist and one day she gave in, she submitted herself to the GENI.

Was she sick? Was she schizophrenic? Was she supposed to be

declared incompetent to stand trial? How, and if at all, are Jung's teachings helpful today, in shedding light on this human tragedy? I will return to these questions later in my talk.

Modern psychiatry began with the French Revolution and probably the first modern Psychiatrist was the French revolutionary physician August Pinel. Being a man in the spirit of his time, Pinel believed that the natural human condition is to be free, i.e. to be responsible for one's fate, to be able to make choices and to give meaning to one's life. Mad ones, the so called Lunatics, were those who, due to a brain disease, became alienated from their true nature. Due to their disease, he claimed, they became unable to decide on their future. According to Pinel, treating the alienated is not only curing their brain disease but helping them to become real human beings again, free people. With this ideology in mind the first modern psychiatric hospitals were founded.

In a way we are all Pinel's followers today, but only to some extent. We all believe that for someone to be mentally ill, there must be an underlying brain pathology, a certain inherited vulnerability, but we tend to disregard the other aspects of Pinel's insights.

Nowadays, when a person dear to us is afflicted with a serious disease, take cancer for example, we all encourage them to fight for their health, to be brave and go through painful treatments. A strong spirit, so we believe, will make the difference in many cases (unfortunately not always) between a terminal disease, and, more and more often, a serious but treatable condition. When a person dear to us is diagnosed with schizophrenia, most of us will have pity on them and on their relatives, we will look upon them as a victim of their brain pathology and at the most, we will encourage them to comply with the doctors' advice, take medications etc. We do not tend to encourage them to fight for their sanity.

On this aspect of schizophrenia, it is so refreshing to recall Jung's teachings.

The 21st century research in the field of mental illness is characterized by enormous human efforts, the investment of enormous financial resources and breathtaking discoveries in areas such as human genetics, biochemistry, epidemiology and imaging. But does our widened understanding of brain functioning in health and in disease have sufficient impact on the destiny of the individual?

Before taking a short "Tour d'Horizon" of the current state of the art in the field of schizophrenia, let us remind ourselves once more of the Jungian perspective.

The term schizophrenia was coined by Bleuler in 1908 at the Burgholzli hospital in Zurich. This term was a reaction to the "Dementia Praecox Syndrome" coined by his contemporary colleague Kraepelin, because, to quote Bleuler: "Today we include patients whom we would neither call 'demented' nor exclusively victims of deterioration in early life". The term he referred to was a disease process characterized by destruction of the internal connections of the personality – a specific alteration of thinking, feeling and relation to the external world. In the course of the disease, the personality loses its unity and the integration of different complexes is lacking. The course of the disease is at times chronic, at times marked by intermittent attacks which can stop or retrograde at any stage but does not permit a full "restitutio ad integrum". Bleuler discerned between fundamental symptoms in the areas of thinking, feeling and volition and secondary (compensatory?) symptoms as delusions and hallucinations.

During these years Bleuler worked with two young assistants, Jung and Binswanger. The latter was the founding father of existential analysis. Little wonder that working together in these formative years Jung and Binswanger influenced each other reciprocally, and the footprints of existentialist thinking is to be found in many of Jung's later works, particularly in the field of psychoses in which they worked together and further developed Bleuler's insights. For Jung, the research and understanding of the psychotic process is fundamental in the formation and the consolidation of Analytical Psychology. His papers on the field of schizophrenia are spread over all his productive years from 1907 till 1958. For Jung, schizophrenia resulted from an "Abaissement du Niveau Mental" a lowering of the consciousness threshold caused by a peculiar "Faiblesse de la Volonte" (notions borrowed from Jannet). This weakening of willpower expresses itself in the way that a train of thoughts is not carried out to its logical conclusion, but is interrupted by strange contents that are insufficiently inhibited. As a result of this lowering of consciousness, complex-contents take over, and the predominance of ego consciousness is endangered. In contrast to neurotic conditions where complexes maintain a connection to the ego and the unity of the personality is maintained, in schizophrenia this connection can be completely lost. In schizophrenia the disconnected complexes will never reintegrate to the psychic totality or, if they can join together in remission, it will be like "a mirror broken into splinters

Some important essentials regarding Jung's theory of schizophrenia: the lowering of the level of consciousness reaches depths which are rarely reached in neurotic conditions while releasing, discharging and constellating deep, archetypal, collective materials which were inhibited and suppressed by the ego. Naturally, these conditions remind us of dreaming, particularly of "big dreams" experienced on the cross-roads of our existence. And indeed much similarity exists between psychosis and dreaming. It was Jung's original contribution to understanding psychosis as a dream without sleep, or to put it in his own words: "The dreamer is normally insane, or that insanity is a dream which has replaced consciousness". An example of a fragment from a dream and a fragment from the narrative of an acutely psychotic patient will show the similarity:

> "...Then I am with S. and other unknown girls in some kind of a new house, modern, rich, and everything (the rooms, ceiling etc.) is round. Between the rooms there are no doors, just glass and everything is transparent. Suddenly, I don't know what happens but I am alone. On the floor there are some triangular elaborate glass stones and I realize that they are not from this world. They are a little bit raised above the floor and activated by my movements. They see me. When I pass nearby they begin to rotate and then break into thousands of sharp glass splinters in the room. I must flee to another room. I realized the stones were evil and they aimed at killing me. I tried to run away and while running I activated more and more stones. I was running from room to room activating more and more glass stones. I felt exhausted moving from room to room and I felt I was going to die".
>
> "... And every night D. (my husband), as if putting S. (my son) to bed, he kills him, and in the morning resurrects him".

Indeed, without knowing the context it will not be easy to guess what is what.

The schizophrenic complex has its peculiarities: elements of a normal or neurotic complex are well-developed, even hypertrophied on account of their heightened energic value. The Schizophrenic complex is characterized by a peculiar deterioration and disintegration, leaving the field of attention undisturbed. It looks as if in schizophrenia the complexes are destroying themselves by distorting their own contents. These complexes do not seem to draw energy from other mental processes, but devour their own energy, subsiding their own foundations and leaving the personality impoverished (or residual, to put it in modern words). Whereas the neurotic dissociation never loses its systematic character, schizophrenia shows a picture of unsystematic randomness in which continuity of meaning is often mutilated to the point of unintelligibility. The picture of the personality dissociation in schizophrenia is different from what is seen in other situations – the split off figures assume grotesque, persecutory or highly exaggerated names and characters. They do not cooperate with the ego-consciousness and often torment it. There is an apparent chaos of visions and voices and characters – overwhelming and strange. In schizophrenia the abaissement reaches a degree never heard of in neurosis – the very foundations of the personality are impaired. Normally inhibited contents of the unconscious are now allowed to invade consciousness.

This problem of the lowering of the level of consciousness and the individual's attitude towards it is for me the main lesson to be taken from Jung's teaching:

Any abaissement, one that leads to neurosis means a weakening of the supreme control. A neurosis is a relative dissociation, a conflict between the ego and a resistant force based upon unconscious contents. Every neurotic fights for the supremacy of ego consciousness and for the subjugation of unconscious forces. A patient who allows himself to be swayed by the intrusion of strange contents from the unconscious, a patient who identifies with, and does not fight with, or is even fascinated by the morbid elements exposes himself to the suspicion of Schizophrenia (Being fascinated by regression!). The abaissement can reach an extreme degree where the ego loses all power (CW 3: 516).

A short illustration to emphasize this point: M., a young professional in his late thirties was referred to me a few months after the birth of his first born son. He had previously accompanied his wife to the maternity room. The delivery was complicated and evolved to a forceps procedure. He witnessed the gynecologist in his work with his hands inside his wife's body. He saw the blood. Little by little, he felt more and more humiliated, he felt his wife was being defiled. He could not be intimate with her anymore, he began to develop strange and hostile beliefs towards male gynecologists, he had murderous drives towards his wife's doctor and began to walk around his house considering to attack him, he had recurring visions of his wife being torn to pieces in the hospital, and more and more felt the urge to save society from what he perceived as perverted wicked gynecologists.

And yet he felt something went wrong, and whenever he felt overwhelmed by his visions and by his aggressive impulses he would bite himself, make himself bleed, so that the physical pains would weaken his phantasies and put him back in touch with reality. One day he was so tormented by inner destructive powers that he had to leave his office. He sat in a public garden biting himself and talking loudly to himself. As he attracted attention, he was approached by a policeman who wanted to refer him to the nearest psychiatric emergency room. Luckily for him, he managed to avoid being hospitalized.

We can imagine that had he been admitted to hospital, he would have been put under heavy surveillance, heavily medicated, probably diagnosed, and in a serious danger of initiating the schizophrenic path.

I will come back to M. as well as to the first patient I mentioned, later on in my talk.

Now to what is schizophrenia in the "era of the brain", and to the actual research endeavors.

As a definition, schizophrenia is a devastating psychiatric syndrome with a median lifetime morbid risk of 7.2 per 1000. The age of onset is typically in adolescence or early adulthood with onset after the fifth decade and in childhood both being rare. All cause mortality is elevated approximately 2.6-fold for patients with schizophrenia, with excess deaths mainly from suicide during the early phase of the disorder, and later from cardiovascular complications. Schizophrenia commonly has a chronic course, albeit with fluctuating patterns and cognitive disability. Its hallmark is psychosis, mainly characterized by positive symptoms, particularly hallucinations and delusions, frequently accompanied by negative (deficit) symptoms such as reduced emotions, speech and interest, and by disorganization of speech and behavior.

DSM V Schizophrenia

2 or more of the following, for a significant portion of time during a month period:

- Delusions

- Hallucinations

- Disorganized speech

- Grossly disorganized or catatonic behavior

- Negative symptoms

- Social/occupational dysfunction

- Duration of at least 6 months

Picture 1

The slide shows us the current DSM definition of the syndrome, showing how far we are today from the original Bleulerian definition. The original definition looked upon delusions and hallucinations as secondary, not necessary attributes of the disease, in contrast to the four fundamental symptoms (Autism, Association, Ambivalence and Affect). For Jung, the secondary symptoms are to be understood as having a psychogenic origin. As to the fundamental ones, he argued with himself whether they should be looked upon as the result of a specific inborn constitutional vulnerability or as being the result of "... An initial emotion which gives rise to metabolic alterations. These emotions seem to be accompanied by chemical processes that cause specific temporary or chronic disturbances or lesions". (Letter to the chairman of a symposium on Chemical Concepts of Psychosis held at the second International Congress for Psychiatry in Zurich September 1-7,1957).

Is schizophrenia an inherited condition?

Familial Risk Factors	
Population	Prevalence (%)
General population	1.0
Non twin sibling of a schizophrenic patient	8.0
Child with one schizophrenic parent	12.0
Dizygotictwin of a schizophrenic patient	12.0
Child of two schizophrenic parents	40.0
Monozygotic twin of a schizophrenic patient	47.0

Picture 2

Bearing in mind familial risk factors, it is little wonder that the deciphering of the human genome yielded hopes to uncover the underlying secrets of schizophrenia. Up to today, over 1000 genes have been tested for association with the disease. The hope is that finding one gene or an association of genes would give way to identifying a specific protein which is in the background of the disturbance. As the research deepens, it becomes more and more clear how difficult it is to investigate the condition we call schizophrenia. On clinical grounds, it shares clinical features with a range of other psychiatric disorders and needs to be diagnosed with high accuracy. On the other hand, the transcription of proteins is much more complicated than previously predicted, even if genes involved with psychiatric illness are identified. As much as still is to be learned from the developing human genetics, we should keep in mind that even between monozygotic twins, sharing exactly the same genetic load, there is only less than 50% concordance for schizophrenia and moreover, most of the schizophrenic patients do not have a first degree sick relative.

The developing field of brain imaging is a second area which raises high expectations. The living structure and the functioning brain, seen in real time, are a challenge to the hope of understanding "what went wrong".

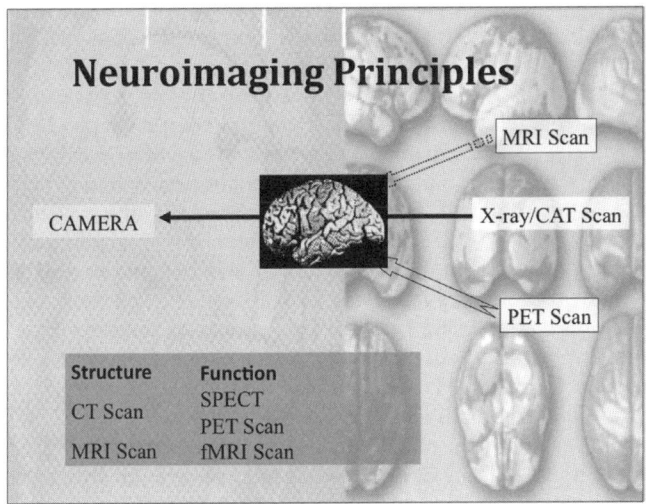

Picture 3

The principal techniques used investigate either structure or function. The first findings, dating from the eighties and nineties with the introduction of the CT scan, showed the enlargement of the intra-cerebral ventricles and the atrophy of the grey matter in chronic schizophrenics compared to healthy subjects. These findings raised numerous objections. It was not clear whether these structural findings were the cause or the effect of the psychotic process. They may even have been the result of years of psychotropic medications.

Other techniques aimed at demonstrating the functioning brain include the fMRI with which, for example, we can detect functional differences between hallucinating and non-hallucinating healthy controls. It is clearly observed from the images that additional neuronal centers are activated in the hallucinatory subjects. Yet the same question remains: Is the brain executing "an order" given by a higher hierarchical function, the way a motor neuron is activated to initiate a movement, but the decision to execute the order comes from elsewhere, or is there a detectable defect in the functioning brain tissue initiating perceptions without external stimuli. One more technique is the PET scan, demonstrating differences in the level of metabolism of different centers of the brain activated during different processes.

So, we actually have ways of beginning to grasp the functioning brain, but whether these findings neglect the patient by concentrating on his/her brain or will it help us to understand psychotics is still to be found out.

A new generation of psychotropic drugs appeared on the market at the beginning of the nineties. They were supposed to be the next pharmacological revolution, after the first one, which took place in the fifties of the last century, with the introduction of the first modern neuroleptic drug. They acted on new categories of neuro-transmitters and were expected to be more efficient and almost lacking side-effects. Their launch was accompanied by a worldwide aggressive campaign by the pharmaceutical companies, with abundant money and gifts (more or less under disguise) distributed to institutions and psychiatrists to encourage their introduction. This Second Generation of Anti psychotics, albeit much more expensive, have become nowadays the first line of treatment. New classes of side-effects, not encountered before, emerged. No more the Parkinsonian patients so typical in the old psychiatric wards, but more obese patients nowadays, in risk to develop Diabetes, Hyperlipidemias, and Cardio Vascular complications. Two major studies, the CATIE in the US and the EUFEST in Europe, financed by public funds devoid of commercial interests, show the equal efficacy of First and Second generation anti psychotic drugs leaving the clinician and the patient with the choice of the least desirable side effects.

PANSS total score over 12 months follow-up

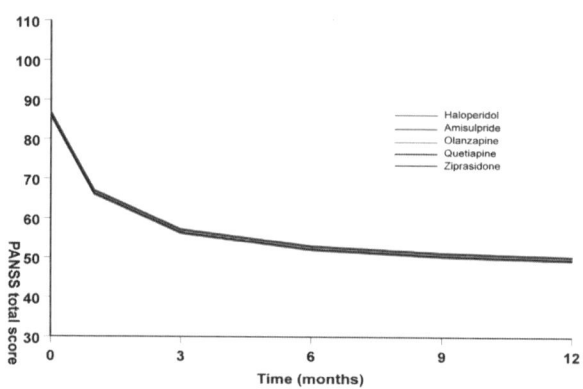

Picture 4 (see color version on CD)

Common to all these research endeavors to connect brain sciences with mental disease is the effort to formulate structures and categories – biological or clinical, in contrast with psychoanalysis, which keeps looking for meaning and for the personal.

Among all those afflicted with psychotic tendencies, who will become schizophrenic and what lesson should we keep in mind in 2013 from Jung's teachings?

The prevalence of psychosis exceeds by far the prevalence of schizophrenia. It is astonishing to see how close this modern observation is to Jung's observation. In 1957, five years after the psychopharmacological revolution he writes: "The number of latent and potential psychoses is astoundingly large in comparison with the manifest cases. Without being able to give exact statistics, I reckon it at 10:1" (CW 3: 558).

The problem is who, among those with a specific vulnerability, will become schizophrenic and who will remit.

At this point I wish to share my personal experience of over thirty years as a practicing psychiatrist working intensively with schizophrenics. I believe that schizophrenia is the disease of the poor and the unprivileged members of society. The typical schizophrenic patient (and, of course, not everyone) will be a young man or woman, generally coming from a disruptive family, often having just one active and present parent, the parent often being unemployed, alcoholic or weak, belonging to a low socio economic status, often originating from an immigrant family either from a different culture or a victim of urbanization, often with minor criminal offences, often experiencing with drugs mainly OTC drugs, often with minor neurological deficits (like Attention Deficits or similar), usually not being able to afford good therapy, but, and most important, without hopes for a better future and without motivation to struggle for his/her sanity. Such a person, being probably constitutionally born with an inherited vulnerability, can one day, in reaction to stress or to a life event, decompensate to an acute psychosis or to a subclinical (prodromal) one. From this point on, the fight for the supremacy of ego consciousness, the recruiting of willpower against the "Faiblesse De La Volonte", so beautifully described by Jung, must be based on the perspectives one could expect from regaining the reality testing, i.e. from meeting life. What does his/her future offer? In a competitive, technologically based, stratified society, when one feels unadapted; it is so tempting to give in and to submit to the lure of the collective unconscious.

Large epidemiological surveys sustain this thesis. Good epidemiological surveys are based on draft board registries like the Swedish one. The Israeli National Draft Board registry is very illuminating as it combines assessment of all adolescents with the national registry of psychiatric hospitalization. We can learn from it that a previous non-psychotic psychiatric diagnosis predisposes up to a certain degree an upcoming diagnosis of schizophrenia. More illuminating is the next picture (Picture 5) demonstrating that the lower the socio economic background, the higher the chance to be hospitalized and diagnosed with schizophrenia.

SES and Risk of Hospitalization fc Schizophrenia

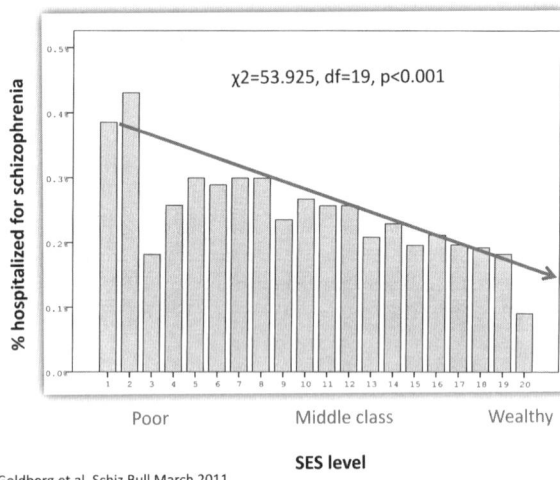

Goldberg et al, Schiz Bull March 2011

Picture 5

Being an immigrant, and furthermore, being an immigrant from a distant society, will be a risk factor as well

Immigration and Risk of Schizophrenia: Significant Cultural Issues

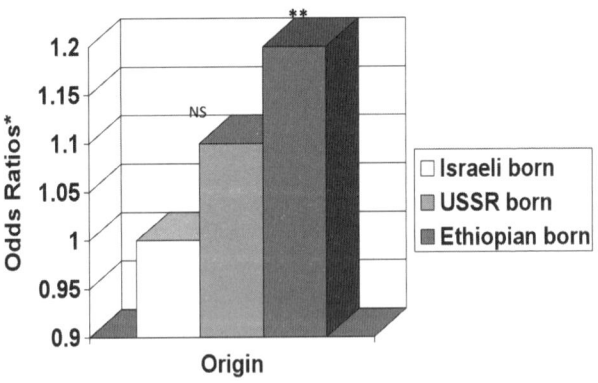

*Adjusted for education & SES **P<0.05   Weiser et al, Psych Med 2007

Picture 6

Being an immigrant from former USSR to Israel could be a risk factor for mental disease but being an immigrant from rural Ethiopia and having to adjust to a very different way of living would be much more dangerous.

Back to the patients with whom I opened this presentation. M., the young professional who accompanied his wife to the maternity room and decompensated to psychosis soon afterwards, is by all means a courageous man. He fights for his ego consciousness, struggles painfully to remain in touch with reality and has fairly good chances for his future. On the other hand, M. is Israeli born, he lives and works in the environment and in the language in which he grew up, he was brought up in a good enough functioning family, he is married and has an average income. Maybe the most important additional factor is that he is lucky to be able to afford a reasonable good continuous therapy.

The young Bedouin woman is in a totally different situation, for her ego consciousness means facing an unbearable situation. For her, there is no way back and even if there was a way, she wouldn't take it. For her, the images of the collective unconscious, even when tormenting, are a better alternative.

The lessons to be learnt from Jung's heritage in the field of treating psychosis are multi-faceted. Even inside our community, and surely in the general public, Jung is looked upon as being much of a mystic, a spiritual and religious thinker. The other aspects of his teachings, his being a sharp and well-grounded clinician are often forgotten and neglected. Sometimes he might have been overly optimistic by asserting, for example in 1957: "It is now about fifty years since I became convinced, through practical experience that schizophrenic disturbances could be treated and cured by psychological means" (CW 3: 559). Even so, now in the "Era of the Brain", when we can look at and observe the functioning brain in real time, when the human genetic code divulges its secrets, when we look upon mental disease through the perspective of statistics, clusters of symptoms, cost-effectiveness, when we look at the homogenous and not at the particular, it is especially invigorating for the therapist to remember Jung's words in 1939:

> The other fact that impressed me is the discovery I made when I began my psychotherapeutic practice: I was amazed at the number of schizophrenics whom we almost never see in psychiatric hospitals. These patients insist upon treatment and I found myself, Bleuler's loyal disciple, trying my hand on cases we never would have dreamed of touching if we had them in the clinic, cases unmistakably schizophrenic even before treatment. I felt hopelessly unscientific in treating them at all – and after the treatment I was told that they could never have been schizophrenic (CW3: 539).

and Jung continues :

Even if I am not very hopeful about a patient, I try to give him as much psychology as he can stand, because I have seen plenty of cases where the later attacks were less severe and the prognosis was better as a result of increased psychological understanding (Ibid).

There are, of course, limitations to Jung's understanding of schizophrenia. For example, he never elaborated on the peculiarity of the schizophrenic complex, how and why it is so different, energically, from the over inflated neurotic complex, and why it is self-devouring. He never elaborated on the reasons for the alienation one feels from his/her surroundings luring them to give up. But he emphasized the central place of one's responsibility to one's mental sanity, and the respect we should all have for those who do not let themselves be swayed away by the intrusion of those strange contents stemming from the unconscious.

Bibliography

Jung C.G. (1939) "The Psychogenesis Of Schizophrenia", CW 3 (516)
Jung C.G. (1958) "Schizophrenia", CW3 (558)
Jung C.G. (1958) "Schizophrenia", CW 3 (559)
Jung C.G. (1939) "The Psychogenesis Of Schizophrenia", CW3 (539)

Panel
From Copenhagen to the Consulting Room:
Complementarity and Synchronicity

"The Who, What, and We of Synchronicity"

Beverley Zabriskie

(JPA, USA)

In April, 1932, quantum physics' best and brightest gathered in Copenhagen at their magnetic center, Niels Bohr's Institute of Theoretical Physics (Serge, 2007).

It was a wondrous and potentially terrible year for physics. It was also the year Wolfgang Pauli consulted C. G. Jung.

The Danish scientist, Bohr, had already presented his model of the atom's interior as a planetary system. The Austrian, Wolfgang Pauli, had gone beyond the three measurable dimensions of height, breadth and depth with his breakthrough theory of the electron spin as an invisible fourth.

Bohr's Principle of Complementarity had been applied to physics in Heisenberg's Uncertainty principle, shifting deterministic notions of cause and effect toward convergences with multiple probabilities. As the framing, and hence the framer of an experiment affected the results, to observe and to experiment was also to effect, requiring the exercise of more "choice and sacrifice" in Pauli's terms. The who acting on the what was an active intervention of mind with matter.

With his particular mix of observation, cognition, imagination and intuition, in 1930, Pauli had made a quantum leap by declaring the existence of a new elementary particle, the neutrino. As it was decades before the neutrino was traced, Pauli admitted: "I have done a terrible thing. I have postulated a particle that cannot be detected." (Hirsch, Pas, Porod, p. 42, 2013).

A truly terrible process had begun just months before the 1932 gathering, when the neutron was detected by scientists in Cambridge. Nuclear energy would soon be released from matter in the first artificial disintegration of the atomic nucleus, leading to the dread fallouts of atomic and nuclear bombs.

Without full consciousness of the negative parallels they were evoking, as 1932 was the centenary year of Goethe's death, the scientists in Copenhagen, mindful they were at the cutting edge of penetrating matter, chose Faust to parody their professional circle. In their production, Niels Bohr/the Lord argues with Pauli/Mephisto who is seeking his version of Faust's Gretchen/Margaret anima as the neutrino, that elusive sub-atomic particle Pauli had claimed. While a featured character, Pauli himself was not present on the stage, in the audience, or in Copenhagen. (Segre, pp.44-56, 2007) Dealing with his elusive anima issues and personal explosiveness, he had recently contacted the eminent Swiss psychiatrist C. G. Jung.

Jung had also posited unobservable background forms, the archetypes, as intimations of inborn dispositions, nodal points of inter-related psychic energies, expectation values which Pauli later saw as "statistical laws with primary probabilities" (von Franz, 1992, pp. 245-252). In 1930, the same year Pauli affirmed the existence of the neutrino beyond the limits of experiment, Jung ended his illuminated journal, the Red Book, with just one word on the main text's last page: *Möglichkeit – possibility.*

As matters of psyche were entering physics, and the physics of the brain was being explored in depth psychology, there were abundant parallels and synchronicities, a-causal connections, between the themes in Copenhagen and those emanating from Zurich. Indeed, Jung's 1932 letters read as psychological riffs on Bohr's conference themes. In one letter, Jung noted that psychological events are bound up with the organic nervous system, so it

> is simply impossible to imagine any experimental set-up which could prove that the psyche exists independently of living matter. This is not to say that it could not exist without matter, since we also take it for granted that matter exists without psyche, doubtful as this appears in the light of the latest finding of quantum physics (Adler, vol.I, pp. 87-88).

Placing mind on the spectrum of organic matter, Jung admitted: "I almost believe that the real history of the human mind is a rhizome phenomenon." (Adler, vol.I, p.102)

In quantum physics, time does not exist. In 1932, addressing the fluidity of psychic time, and Jung too was evoking Goethe's masterpiece:

> My mother drew my attention to Faust when I was about 15 years old....It seems to me that one cannot meditate enough about Faust... It is as much the future as the past and therefore the most living present (Adler, vol.I, pp. 88-89).

In both quantum physics and depth psychology, the categories of time and space were being explored as plastic categories of perception rather than as fundamental, universal laws. From the insights of his psychological types theory, Jung was suggesting that our sense of time depends on which function is active:

Because it is tied to the timeless, the inferior function never wants to affirm the world of the moment, the world of time, since it would rather cling on to timelessness (Adler, vol. 1, p. 94).

In December of 1932, Jung relativized cause and effect in the time sequence of an analytic process, asserting the predominant effect of what today we might term neural coupling, when the present moment of meeting overcomes what is transferred from the past: "Everything depends on how you strike the patient as a human being. In the end the personality is the most powerful therapeutic agent." (Adler, vol.1, p. 112).

The relationship that began in 1932 between Jung and Pauli evolved over three decades. Both wittingly and implicitly, Pauli embodied an energy current between himself, Bohr and Jung. While such figures as Goethe, Schopenhauer, and Lao Tse were referenced, the influence of the American philosopher William James was most apparent. James' notion of the complementary – in the relations among internal, partial selves, and the inter-relationship between the explorations of unconscious dynamics in psyche and invisible forms of physical matter – were in play. James' thesis informs Bohr's Principle of Complementarity, Heisenberg's Uncertainty Principle, Pauli and Jung's Synchronicity. James' influence is acknowledged in Jung's theory of complexes, the transcendent function, the metaphor of the alchemical *coniunctio*, of individuation as integration of one's many parts, and indeed of psyche as a multiplicity within a unity (Zabriskie, 2001, p. xxix).

In 1949, Jung wrote Markus Fierz that Pauli "prompted" him to the *"putting together of my thoughts on the concept of synchronicity."*

Since physicists are the only people nowadays who would be able to deal with such a concept successfully, it is from a physicist that I hope to meet with critical understanding although, as you will see, the empirical basis seems to lie wholly in the realm of psychic phenomena (Adler, vol.1, p.530).

The challenge to magical thinking of cause and effect is present in both his theory of synchronicity and in Jung's confrontation with the human projection of the God image. In 1955, he wrote to Upton Sinclair:

Soon, a little book of mine ... with the physicist Prof. W. Pauli will come out in English. It is even more shocking than Job, but this time to the scientist, not the theologian. It deals with the "random phenomenon" of extrasensory perception, especially its theory. ... The public reaction will be even worse than in the case of Job (Adler, vol. 2, p. 232).

Jung and Pauli engaged in an immediate, emotional, intellectual, neural coupling, with Bohr in the background. Jung and Pauli also shared Bohr's paper on Light and Life. Pauli often dreamt of Bohr, as a complementary to Jung.

As far as we know, Jung and Bohr never met. Their tangential connection was akin to the "quantum weirdness" of physic pairings, of "spooky action at a distance." Jung made direct and indirect self-comparisons to Bohr: "when you observe the phenomenon of the interior of the atom, you find that your observation disturbs the thing you observe, and if you go on observing, you observe the thing that disturbs, you discover the psyche. (1998, ZA, vol. I, p. 244) In 1952, he wrote:

> Effects can be empirically established whose cause is described hypothetically as "archetype", just as in physics effects can be established whose cause is assumed to be the "atom" (which is merely a model.) Nobody has ever seen an archetype, and nobody has ever seen at atom. But the former is known to produce numinous effects and the latter explosions. When I say "atom" I am talking of the model made of it; when I say "archetype", I am talking of ideas corresponding to it, but never of the thing-in-itself (Adler, vol. 2, p. 54).

He continued:

> It would never occur to a physicist that he has bagged the bird with his atomic model (for instance Neils Bohrs' planetary system). He is fully aware that he is handling a variable schema or model which merely points to unknowable facts. This is scientific gnosis, such as I also pursue. Only it is news to me that such knowledge is accounted "metaphysical" (Adler, vol. 2, p. 54).

One year before his death, Jung again evoked Niels Bohr. In his June, 1960 response to Buber's allegation that his ontological denial reduced God to an object, Jung wrote:

> If Niels Bohr compares the model of atomic structure with a planetary system, he knows it is merely a model of a transcendent and unknown reality, and if I talk of the God-image, I do not deny a transcendental reality. I merely insist on the psychic reality of the God-complex or the God-image, as Niels Bohr proposes the analogy of a planetary system. He would not be as dumb as to believe that his model is an exact and true replica of the atom. No empiricist in his senses would believe his models to be the eternal truth itself. He knows too well how many changes any kind of reality undergoes in becoming a conscious representation (Adler, vol 2, p. 572).

With synchronicity, Jung placed the psyche in the workings of the universe as an agent in linking random phenomenon, in creating a narrative which allows a perspective of interconnected meaning, as "an act of creation in time."

Today, insights about synchronicity as a product of mind in relation to outer patterns come from artists, and scientists, writers and musicians. When Jung's Red Book was chosen for the 2013 Venice Biennale, its artistic director Massimiliano Gioni commented:

> This show will deal with our age of hyper-connectivity, by looking at what goes on in our heads rather than online. It is about the synchronicity of the past, the present and the future. (Vogel, New York Times, June 2, 2013).

Tobias Meyer, Sotheby's Director, called this international exhibit "a game changer":

> "It finally addresses the theory of contemporary art that is based on Jung, on the unearthing of the subconscious," he explained. "The art world right now is all about Pop and global culture and dispersing images via the Internet whereas this is about exploring the deepest sense of oneself and the genesis of art" (Vogel, New York Times, May 23, 2013).

In a 1936 *Zarathustra Seminar*, Jung opined that "the speculative modern physicist will surely come into very close contact with the psychologist." (1998,ZA, vol. 2, p. 928) Pauli wrote Jung:

> Just as physics seeks completeness, your analytical psychology seeks a home. … psychology… leads an esoteric, special existence beyond the fringe of …the academic world. But this is how the archetype of the coniunctio is constellated. Whether and when this coniunctio will be realized I do not know, but I am in no doubt at all that this would be the finest fate that could happen to both physics and psychology (Meier, 2001, Letter 62, May 27th, 1953)

From physics, as you will read, our panelist Harald Atmanspacher is making this happen. In the June 2013 *Scientific American*, his comrade-trouble-maker-in-arms, Christopher Fuchs refers to the Born Rule of "how to calculate the probability of a quantum event using the wave function" in strikingly psychological terms.

> Fuchs proposes 'that the wave function is just a tool that tells observers how to calculate their personal beliefs, or probabilities, about the quantum world around them. By interpreting the wave function as personal degrees of belief, it gives precise, mathematical meaning to Bohr's intuition that physics concerns what we can say about nature' (von Baeyar, 2013 p.51).

Fuchs posits that

'every measurement set by an experimenter's free will, the world is shaped just a little as it participates in a kind of moment of birth.' In this way, we become active contributors to the ongoing creation of the universe (von Baeyar, 2013, p.51).

Now, physicists pursue branes and strings in the multidimensional fabrics of the universe, while analysts pursue the capacity for interconnectedness with a synthesizing self and synaptic brain, living on a plane of what and who. Jung quotes the Paraclesian alchemist/ physician Gerhard Dorn:

But no man truly know himself unless first he see and know by zealous meditation, … what rather than who he is, on whom he depends, and whose he is, and to what end he was made and created, and by whom and through whom (CW 14, para 684).

In modern terms, we are informationally coupled with the various forms of life in our universe.

In a contemporary play, Michael Frayn's *Copenhagen,* Bohr's character addresses Heisenberg:

We put man back at the centre of the universe… It starts with Einstein. He shows that measurement, on which the whole impossibility of science depends – measurement … (is) a human act, carried out from a specific point of view in time and space, from the one particular viewpoint of a possible observer. Then, here in Copenhagen in those three years in the mid-twenties we discover that there is no precisely determinable objective universe. That the universe exists only as a series of approximations. Only within the limits determined by our relationship with it. Only through the understanding lodged inside the human head (Frayn, 1998, pp. 73-74).

References

Adler, G. Ed. (1974-1975) Letters of C. G. Jung. Vol. 1 and 2. Princeton. Princeton University Press.

Frayn, M.(1998) *Copenhagen.* London: Methuan Drama.

Hirsch, Pas, Porod. (2013) "Ghostly Beacons of New Physics." *Scientific American Magazine,* April 2013

Jung, C. G. (1952) "Synchronicity: An Acausal Connecting Principle." CW 8. (1955-56) *Mysterium Coniunctionis.* CW 14

Jung, C. G., Jarrett, J. L. Ed. (1998). Jung's *Seminar on Nietzsche's Zarathustra* (Abridged ed.). Princeton, N.J.: Princeton University Press.

Segre, Gino. (2007) *Faust in Copenhagen: A Struggle for the Soul of Physics.* New York: Viking. Penguin Group.

Vogel. C. (2013) "New Guide in Venice", *New York Times*, May 23. (2013) "Ripples of Rumination" *New York Times,* June 2

von Baeyer, H.C.(2013) "Quantum Weirdness? It's All in Your Mind" June 2013; *Scientific American* Magazine

von Franz, M.L. (1992)Psyche and Matter. Boston & London, Shambhala.

Zabriskie, B. (2001) "A Meeting of Rare Minds" Preface in *Atom and Archetype. The Pauli/Jung Letters 1932-1958.* Meier, C. Ed. Princeton: Princeton University Press.

Psychophysical Correlations, Synchronicity and Meaning

Harald Atmanspacher

(Collegium Helveticum, Zurich)
(Faculty member of the Jung Institute Zurich)

Conceiving the mind-matter distinction in terms of an epistemic split of a psychophysically neutral domain implies correlations between mind and matter as a direct and generic consequence. It is important, though, to stress right at the outset that these correlations are not due to causal interactions (in the sense of efficient causation as usually looked for in science) between the mental and the material. In a dual-aspect framework of thinking it would be wrong to interpret mind (or mental states) as directly caused by matter (or material states) or vice versa.

Synchronicity

In a condensed form, two (or more) seemingly accidental, but not necessarily simultaneous events are called synchronistic if the following three conditions are satisfied.

- Each pair of synchronistic events includes an internally conceived and an externally perceived component.

- Any presumption of a direct causal relationship between the events is absurd or even inconceivable.

- The events correspond with one another by a common meaning, often expressed symbolically.

The first criterion makes clear that synchronistic phenomena are psychophysical phenomena, intractable when dealing with mind or matter alone. The second criterion emphasizes the inapplicability of causation in the narrow sense of a conventional cause-and-effect-relation. And the third criterion suggests the concept of meaning as a constructive way to characterize mind-matter correlations.

Since synchronistic phenomena are not necessarily temporally "synchronous" (in the sense of "simultaneous"), synchronicity is a somewhat misleading term. For this reason Pauli preferred to speak of "meaningful correspondences" under the influence of an archetypal "acausal ordering". He considered Jung's synchronicity as a particular instance of such an acausal ordering which cannot be set up intentionally. In contrast, the mathematical notion of "blind" chance (referring to stochastically accidental events) might be considered as the limiting case of a meaningless correspondence.

What Pauli here postulates is a kind of lawful regularity beyond both deterministic and statistical laws, based on the notion of meaning and, thus, entirely outside the natural sciences of his time and also, more or less, of today. It remains to be explored how this key issue of meaning can be implemented in an expanded world view not only comprising, but rather exceeding both psychology and physics. A comprehensive substantial account of psychophysical phenomena needs to address them beyond the distinction of the psychological and the physical.

For the mindset of a psychologist like Jung, the issue of meaning is of primary significance anyway. For a long time, Jung insisted that the concept of synchronicity should be reserved for cases of distinctly numinous character, when the experience of meaning takes on existential dimensions. With this understanding synchronistic correlations would be extremely rare, thus contradicting their supposedly generic nature. Only in later years, Jung opened up toward the possibility that synchronicity might be a notion that should be conceived as ubiquitous as indicated above

Structural versus Induced Correlations

The development of Pauli's and Jung's views about archetypes and their role in manifesting synchronicities suggests a distinction between two basically different kinds of mind-matter correlations for which we propose the notions of "structural" and "induced" correlations.

Structural correlations refer to the role of archetypes as ordering factors with an exclusively *unidirectional* influence on the material and the mental. They arise due to epistemic splits of the unus mundus, which manifest themselves as correlations at the level of mental and material aspects. Since these correlations are a straightforward consequence of the basic structure of the model, they do not depend on additional contexts. They must be assumed to be persistent, and insofar as they are persistent, they should be empirically reproducible.

Induced correlations refer to the backreaction that changes of consciousness induce in the unconscious and, consequently, in the physical world as well. Likewise, measurements of physical systems induce backreactions in the physical ontic reality, which can lead to changes of mental states. This way, the picture is extended to a *bidirectional* relation. In contrast to structural, persistent correlations, induced correlations depend on all kinds of contexts, so they must be expected to occur only occasionally, and to be evasive and not (easily) reproducible.

While structural correlations define a baseline of ordinary, robust

psychophysical correlations (such as mind-brain correlations or psychosomatic correlations), induced correlations (positive or negative)
may be responsible for alterations and deviations (above or below)
this baseline. Induced positive correlations, above the baseline, could
be characterized as phenomena with overemphasized correlations.
Synchronistic events in the sense Jung proposed originally clearly
belong to this class. Induced negative correlations, below the baseline,
are experienced as dissociative with respect to ordinary baseline
correlations.

It is important to keep in mind that in both induced and structural
correlations there is no direct causal relation from the mental to the
physical or vice versa (i.e. no direct "efficient causation"). The problem
of a direct "causal interaction" between categorically distinct regimes
is thus avoided. Of course, this does not mean that the correlations
themselves are causeless: the cause for structural correlations is the
epistemic split of the unus mundus. The causes for induced correlations are interventions in the conscious mental or local material
domain, whose backeffects on the unus mundus must be expected
to manifest themselves in the complementary domain, respectively.

Intentionality and Meaning

In the definition of synchronicity, the common meaning of mental
and material events figures prominently. However, meaning is a noto-
riously difficult notion, used differently in different areas and contexts.
In a general sense, meaning is a two-place relation between a sign
and what it designates, or a representation and what it represents.
Meaning in this sense is simply a reference relation, in accordance
with the philosophical usage of the term intentionality after Brentano.
What Jung had in mind when he emphasized meaning is different,
however. He did clearly aim at meaning as an element of experience,
not as a formal relationship.

It should be stressed that this kind of meaning, although being
subjectively ascribed (by the experiencing subject), is not completely
arbitrary. It depends on the situation as a whole, likely including
conditions that are not consciously available to the subject. According
to Jung, synchronistic events arise due to constelled archetypal
activity. This activity limits the range of possibly attributable meanings.

In typical situations of "ordinary" structural mind-matter correlations, this formal intentionality is hardly experienced explicitly
– subjects usually "know" the corresponding meaning, but are not
explicitly aware of its phenomenal quality. This is different for induced
mind-matter correlations: the deviation from the ordinary baseline
stimulates that experienced intentionality is incurred. In this case, the

corresponding meaning is distinctly and phenomenally inflicted upon the experiencing subject.

In his concept of synchronicity, Jung emphasized induced mind-matter correlations in the sense of meaningful coincidences, i.e. positive correlations above the ordinary baseline. The approach presented here includes negative correlations below the baseline, whose meaning appears in dissociation events rather than coincidence events. Jungian synchronicities may be regarded as special cases of induced positive mind-matter correlations with large deviations above the baseline.

Exceptional Human Experiences

The rich material of extraordinary psycho-physiological correlations suggests various concrete types of psychophysical correlations. Moreover, a recent statistical analysis of a huge body of documented cases of extraordinary human experiences provides significant evidence that the Pauli-Jung conjecture matches with existing empirical material surprisingly well.

Particularly relevant with respect to the notion of meaning are experiences which refer to the way in which mental and physical states are merged or separated above or below ordinary baseline correlations. In coincidence phenomena ordinarily disconnected elements of self and world appear connected; in dissociation phenomena ordinarily connected elements of self and world appear disconnected.

Coincidence phenomena refer to experiences of positive psychophysical correlations above the persistent ordinary baseline. Typically, these correlations are experienced as acausal meaningful links between mental and material events, e.g. meaningful coincidences such as Jungian "synchronicities". Spatiotemporal restrictions may appear as inefficacious, as in several kinds of "extrasensory perception".

Dissociation phenomena refer to experiences of induced negative mind-matter correlations below the persistent ordinary baseline. For instance, subjects are not in full control of their bodies, or experience autonomous behavior not deliberately set into action. Out-of-body experiences, sleep paralysis and various forms of automatized behavior are among the most frequent phenomena in this class.

In order to assess whether and how these classes are empirically relevant, they have been compared with empirical data from clients seeking advice from the counseling department of the Institute for Frontier Areas of Psychology (Freiburg, Germany). The patterns obtained by factor analyses reflect the subjective views of the clients about their experiences. The collected data yield an exclusively phenomenological classification scheme, not a system for clinical diagnosis.

It turned out that coincidence and dissociation phenomena represent key patterns in the documented material from IGPP clients. An additional study, based on subjects from ordinary population (rather than advice-seeking clients) was recently published by Fach et al. (2013). As expected, the average intensity of their reported experiences is rated significantly lower than for IGPP clients. However, the patterns extracted from the ordinary population sample as well as their relative frequencies are in perfect agreement with the IGPP sample.

Bibliography

Atmanspacher, H. (2012): Dual-aspect monism à la Pauli and Jung. *Journal of Consciousness Studies*, 19(9/10), 96-120.

Atmanspacher, H., and Fach, W. (2013): A structural-phenomenological typology of mind-matter correlations. *Journal of Analytical Psychology* 58, 219–244 (2013). A commentary to this paper by David Tresan and a reply to it by the authors are published subsequently in the same journal issue.

Bauer, E., Belz, M., Fach, W., Fangmeier, R., Schupp-Ihle, C. and Wiedemer, A. (2012): Counseling at the IGPP – An overview. In: *Perspectives of Clinical Parapsychology*, ed. by W.H. Kramer, E. Bauer, and G.H. Hövelmann, Stichting Het Johan Borgman Fonds, Bunnik, 149–167.

Belz, M. and Fach, W. (2012): Theoretical reflections on counseling and therapy for individuals reporting ExE [exceptional experiences]. In: *Perspectives of Clinical Parapsychology*, ed. by W.H. Kramer, E. Bauer, and G.H. Hövelmann, Stichting Het Johan Borgman Fonds, Bunnik, 168–189.

Brentano, F. (1874): *Psychologie vom empirischen Standpunkt*, Leipzig: Duncker & Humblot.

Fach, W. (2011): Phenomenological aspects of complementarity and entanglement in exceptional human experiences. *Axiomathes* 21, 233–247.

Fach, W., Atmanspacher, H., Landolt, K., Wyss, T., and Rössler, W. (2013): A comparative study of exceptional experiences of clients seeking advice and of subjects in an ordinary population. *Frontiers in Psychology* 4:65, 1–10.

Jung, C.G. (1969): On the nature of the psyche, in The Structure and Dynamics of the Psyche. Collected Works, Vol. 8, pp. 159–236, Princeton: University Press.

Jung, C.G., and Pauli, W. (1952): *Naturerklärung und Psyche*, Zürich: Rascher.

Kapur, S. (2003): Psychosis as a state of aberrant salience: A framework linking biology, phenomenology, and pharmacology in schizophrenia. *American Journal of Psychiatry* 160, 13–23.

Kelly, E.W. (2007): Psychophysiological Influence, in Kelly, E.F., Kelly, E.W. et al. (eds.) *Irreducible Mind*, 117–239, Lanham: Rowman and Littlefield.

Meier, C.A. (1975): Psychosomatik in Jungscher Sicht, in Meier, C.A. (ed.) *Experiment und Symbol*, 138–156, Olten: Walter.

Metzinger, T. (2003*): Being No One*, Cambridge, MIT Press,.

Meyenn, K. von (ed.) (1993): Wolfgang Pauli. *Wissenschaftlicher Briefwechsel*, Band III: 1940–1949, Berlin: Springer.

Stubenberg, L. (2010): Neutral monism, in Zalta, E.N. (ed.) *Stanford Encyclopedia of Philosophy*, http://plato.stanford.edu/entries/neutral-monism/.

From Copenhagen to the Consulting Room:
Pauli and Jung in Copenhagen

Suzanne Gieser

(CG Jung foundation, Stockholm, Sweden)

Niels Bohr's Influence on Wolfgang Pauli

Pauli met Niels Bohr for the first time on 22 June 1921 and as a result he was invited to Copenhagen. From 1922 to 23 Pauli studied at the Institute for Theoretical Physics and remained in lifelong contact and deep friendship with Bohr from this point onwards.

Pauli with Bohr's two sons, Christian and Harald 1923

The Institute was built in 1921, and Bohr had planned almost everything from the blackboards to the vacuum pumps. He also had his living quarters and family in the building, which led to a unique learning environment that was characterized by a fluidity of the boundaries between the private and the professional, work and leisure, science and philosophy. How strongly Bohr influenced the lives of his students is shown by the fact that many of them learned to speak and write in Danish, and acquired Danish girlfriends and wives. All this became known as "the Copenhagen spirit". Bohr became a father figure to Pauli and had a great influence on him, as indeed he had on many other young physicists (Pais, 1991; Beller, 1999; Meyenn, 1985; Pauli, 1945/1994).

Pauli also learned to speak and write in Danish. The language even influenced his dreams, one of which he discussed in detail in 1956. Working with Bohr influenced Pauli's philosophy, not only with regards to physics, but also his approach to epistemology and life itself. Pauli said that Bohr taught him "that every true philosophy must actually start off with a paradox" (Pauli to Jung, 27 February 1953, Pauli, 2001). Pauli described how through Bohr he became acquainted with a Kierkegaardian atmosphere. Bohr gave Pauli two books by Kierkegaard, although he didn't get very far in his reading of them.

> I have been in this atmosphere, which *seeks an equilibrium between opposing pairs*, since my earliest youth. /.../ So your remarks /.../, take me back to those days in 1923 when I was working in the laboratory of Niels Bohr. For he used often to quote Schiller's "Sayings of Confucius": "The full mind alone is the clear, and truth dwells in the deeps", to which he attached lengthy philosophical expositions. These culminated in a proposition which he later called "the complementarity between clarity and truth": if an assertion is too clear, then there is something wrong with its accuracy, and if an assertion is true, then its clarity is limited. For every truth also contains in part something unknown, only glimpsed and therefore also a hidden opposite to its conscious meaning. (I now believe that is just what psychologists call "symbol", which does not seem to me to be so very different from what mathematicians call "symbol".) (Goldschmidt, 1990).

In this quotation we can see how Pauli links the influence from Bohr with the ideas of C. G. Jung (See also Gieser, 1995).

Jung in Scandinavia

As far as we know Jung visited Scandinavia once, in October 1937, when he was in Copenhagen for the 9th conference of the International General Medical Society for Psychotherapy. The conference was arranged by Poul Bjerre, the Swede who introduced psychoanalytic and psychodynamic ideas in Sweden, together with his Danish colleague, Oluf Brüel. Bjerre was one of a handful of Swedish doctors who in the 1920s were interested in a wider approach to psychotherapy. Coming from the tradition of hypnosis, Bjerre was a pupil of the famous Otto Wetterstrand. In 1911 he met Freud in Vienna, and as a result he introduced the ideas of Freud, Alfred Adler and C.G. Jung to Swedish audiences. He also developed a method of his own called Psychosynthesis (branded in 1909, not to be confused with Roberto Assagioli's school) and regarded himself as belonging to the anagogic school, which was closer to Jung than to Freud when it came to the view of the unconscious as a creative source of healing. After having difficulties being recognized by the Swedish Medical Society, he joined the *General Medical Society for Psychotherapy,* founded in Germany, in 1926. This was the first professional organization for psychotherapists, in which he became very active from the start. Jung also joined this Society in 1928, and became its president in 1933, when the Nazi regime took over. The Society was later re-organized into an international umbrella organization.

Although the Society had held annual conferences between 1926 and 1931, the catastrophic developments in Germany in the years that followed made this arrangement impossible. This engaged Bjerre a great deal, to the extent that he suggested that a conference should instead be held in Stockholm or elsewhere in Scandinavia. Bjerre worked very hard to organize groups in Scandinavia. This proved difficult, partly due to the conflicts among the different schools of psychoanalysis and psychotherapy.

In 1933 Bjerre managed to assemble the first small Nordic group of Swedish, Norwegian and Danish members (Nordiskt psykoterapeutiskt kollegium NPK).

The Nordic Psychotherapy Team, NPK. From left to right; upper row, third: Egil Rønne-Petersen (Norway), fourth and fifth: Signe and Iwan Bratt (Sweden), lower row: second Johan Irgens Strømme (Norway), third Poul Bjerre (Sweden), fourth Sigurd Næsgaard (Denmark).

However, in 1934 a congress was held in Bad Nauheim at which Jung presented the new umbrella organization. Bjerre realized that a Nordic organization was of little use in this new international society, which only national groups were allowed to join. Bjerre then tried to gather a group of Swedish doctors and create a national Swedish group. He called on his Nordic colleagues to do the same. He finally succeeded in 1936.

The conference of 1936 was cancelled by the Dutch group due to the political developments in Germany. Jung wrote to Bjerre to tell him that he wanted to resign from the presidency, but Bjerre urged him to stay on and pushed his idea of a conference in Copenhagen. With historical hindsight it would have been better if Jung had actually resigned. Finally, aided by his Danish colleague, Oluf Brüel, and the Danish group, a conference was arranged in October 1937. The theme of the conference was "Psychotherapy and General Praxis", which was held at the Domus Medica, the residence of the Danish Medical Society at Amaliegade 5 (Gieser, 2009a).

The 1936 Conference in Copenhagen

Inspired by The Guild of Pastoral Psychology and the Tavistock Clinic, Bjerre founded the Institute for Medical Psychology and Psychotherapy in 1946. The first Swedish Jungian, the theologian Ivar Alm, was active at this Institute for a period. He wrote his doctoral thesis on Jung, went to Berlin and Zürich for lectures and analysis, translated some of Jung's writings and wrote and lectured on Jung in Sweden (Gieser, 2009b).

The Bailey Island and New York Seminars on Pauli's Dreams in 1936 and 1937

When Jung visited Copenhagen he was on his way to the United States. At the beginning of 1937 he was invited to lecture at Yale. In 1936 he was invited to Harvard University. Kristine Mann, Eleanor Bertine and Ester Harding, the three female Jungian pioneers who were then living in the United States, urged him to come and give seminars to their groups. They chose the topic "the individuation process traced through a series of dreams or fantasies", which dealt with a selection of the 410 dreams recorded by Pauli. This was the first time Pauli's dreams had been presented to an English speaking audience. Jung had originally planned to cover 81 of the dreams, but was able to cover only 34 of them during his 5 days in Maine. Although no continuation of the seminar was planned at the time, it seemed natural to continue the seminars on Pauli's dreams when he returned to the United States in 1937. This time, the seminars were held in Manhattan and Jung covered another 33 of the dreams. He closed the seminar by referring to the dreams that he had covered in the Terry lectures, where he had discussed Pauli's dream of the Catholic church, the dream of the solemn house and the vision of the world clock. Jung later decided to publish Pauli's dream series, which at that time had been presented as a study of the *mandala* motif under the title *Psychology and Alchemy* (Jung, 1944). (In my introduction to the publication of these seminars I hope to outline the process that lay behind the change of context to that of alchemy).

Pauli Dreaming in Danish

I would like to end by drawing attention to Pauli's knowledge of Danish and how this became visible in his dreams. In October 1956 Pauli sent a letter to Jung about a couple of his dreams and their interpretation. In one of them Pauli dreamt that Bohr was explaining the difference between the letters v and w to him, and that this had to do with the difference between Danish and English, with the addition that Pauli should not just stick to Danish but move on to English. When Pauli woke up he was excited, and the word *vindue* (window) immediately came into his mind. He embarked on an exposé of how, through different encounters with scholars, he had discovered that the phonetic difference between V and W (pronounced U) had come into English from Old German. Pauli then started to associate with the letter U by stating that he had been using the term "U-field" for the unconscious, and that he had been suppressing it too strongly with the V of rational language. He interpreted Danish as the language of physics, his everyday conscious rational language and English as the language of dreams, with the English w *(pronounced double u)* as a symbol. He thought that the unconscious and the conscious had to resonate together in a new synthesis. He also discovered that the word vindue translated into "wind eye". He concluded that: *The dreams and their images are "Windaugen"(wind eyes) for me: With the resonating of a subliminal pneuma (wind), which is protective and protected, and its synthesis with normal every-day language, it produces in these dreams and images a new type of visual faculty* (Pauli to Jung, 23 October 1956, Meier 2001).

I was reminded of this dream when I visited Hilma af Klint's exhibition in Stockholm in February this year. Her esoteric art predates most modern art. In her early paintings from 1906, which were "channelled" to her through spiritualistic séances, the letters w and u recur. Here w stands for the material world and u for the spiritual world (Klint, Lomas, Rousseau, & Zander, 2013). According to Kuhn (1976, p. 5), in his book on the Esoteric Structure of the Alphabet, in the Hebrew alphabet the letter U together with V represents the descent of spirit into matter, and its return. It is, perhaps, also worth mentioning that both Hilma af Klint's art and Jung's *Red Book* are on display at this year's 55th International Art Exhibition in Venice.

Acknowledgments

Image 1: Pauli with Bohr's two sons, Christian and Harald 1923, with permission from the Pauli archive, CERN.

Image 2: The Nordic Psychotherapy team, NPK with permission from The Poul Bjerre Archive, Stockholm.

Image 3: The 1936 conference in Copenhagen, permission from the Jung family.

Bibliography

Beller, Mara (1999). *Quantum dialogue: the making of a revolution*. Chicago, Ill.: Univ. of Chicago Press.

Meyenn, K. v. (1985). *Niels Bohr 1885-1962: Der Kopenhagener Geist In Der Physik*. Braunschweig: F. Vieweg.

Gieser, Suzanne. (2005). *The Innermost Kernel [electronic resource] : Depth Psychology and Quantum Physics. Wolfgang Pauli's Dialogue with C.G. Jung.* Berlin, Heidelberg: Springer-Verlag Berlin Heidelberg.

Gieser, Suzanne (2009a). *Psykoterapins pionjärer i Sverige*. Stockholm: Proprius.

Gieser, Suzanne (2009b). "Jungintroduktören Ivar Alm", *Coniunctio*. (2000-). Råå: C G Jung föreningen i Skåne.

Goldschmidt, Hermann Levin (1990). *Nochmals DIALOGIK*. Zürich : ETH Stiftung Dialogik.

Jung, C. G. (1953). *The collected works of C.G. Jung, Vol. 12, Psychology and alchemy*. New York: Pantheon.

Klint, Hilma af, Lomas, David, Rousseau, Pascal & Zander, Helmut (2013). *Hilma af Klint: a pioneer of abstraction*. Stockholm: Moderna museet.

Kuhn, A. B. (1976), *The Esoteric Structure of the Alphabet*. Whitefish, MT: Kessinger Publishing, LLC.

Pais, Abraham (1993). *Niels Bohr's times: in physics, philosophy and polity*. 1. pbk ed. Oxford: Oxford Univ. Press.

Pauli, Wolfgang (1994). *Writings on physics and philosophy*. Berlin: Springer

Pauli, Wolfgang (2001). *Atom and archetype: the Pauli/Jung letters, 1932-1958*. Princeton, N.J.: Princeton University Press.

Also, the forthcoming publication of *Dream Symbols of the Individuation Process: Notes of the Seminars given by Jung in Bailey Island and New York, 1936-7* by the Philemon Foundation.

The Cultural Significance of Synchronicity for Jung and Pauli

Roderick Main

(Centre for Psychoanalytic Studies,
University of Essex, UK)

Scientific Rationalism and Its Consequences

In their respective fields of psychology and physics, Carl Jung (1875-1961) and Wolfgang Pauli (1900-1958) were among the most highly honoured thinkers of the twentieth century. Yet both were also deeply critical of the culture in which they trained and worked. In particular, while proudly identifying themselves as scientists, they considered that the rationalistic cast of the dominant science of their day was narrow and dangerous, entraining serious psychological, social, political, and ethical problems. For Jung, science "is based in the main on statistical truths and abstract knowledge and therefore imparts an unrealistic, rational picture of the world" (CW10, par. 498). This leads to a "levelling down" of "not only the psyche but the individual man and, indeed, all individual events whatsoever" (CW10, par. 499). The "statistical world picture" thus "thrust aside the individual in favour of anonymous units that pile up into mass formations" – "organizations", "the abstract idea of the State" – in which the "[t]he goal and meaning of individual life (which is the only *real* life)" are submerged (CW10, par. 499). In Jung's view, the consequences of this "psychological mass-mindedness" (CW10, par. 501) brought about by scientific rationalism show up both in individual pathology, where one-sidedly intellectual patients cut off from their instincts and emotions suffer a sense of "meaninglessness" (CW8, par. 815; cf. pars. 982, 845), and in the social and political spheres where, he argues, mass-mindedness provides the conditions in which totalitarianism can flourish (CW10, pars. 488-516; see also Main, 2004, pp. 117-121, 135-138).

Similarly for Pauli, current science, which for him meant in particular physics, was incomplete because, even when acknowledging the inescapable role of the observer in quantum mechanics, it still excluded feeling, value, psychological reality, and the realm of the non-rational and qualitative generally (see, e.g., Pauli, 1952, pp. 206-208; PJL, pp. 195-196; Gieser, 2005, p. 140). At the individual level, this exclusion fostered a hypertrophy of reason such as, in Pauli's own case, had precipitated the personal crisis that led to his seeking treatment from Jung (Gieser, 2005, pp. 142-154; Miller, 2009, pp. 124-147). At a more social and political level, scientific rationalism resulted in a perilous dissociation of science from morality – a situation epitomised for Pauli by the direct and indirect involvement of physicists in the development of the atom bomb and their complicity thereby in mass murder (Gieser, 2005, pp. 23, 323-324; Miller, 2009, p. 176; cf. PJL, pp. 75-76).

"The Influence of Archetypal Ideas on the Scientific Theories of Kepler"

Jung and Pauli's joint publication *The Interpretation of Nature and the Psyche* (1952) – including Jung's essay "Synchronicity: An Acausal Connecting Principle" and Pauli's essay "The Influence of Archetypal Ideas on the Scientific Theories of Kepler" – was an attempt to address these psychological, social, political, and ethical problems by developing a revised understanding of science and of the relationship between matter and psyche.

Pauli's essay (1952) uses the historical example of the seventeenth-century polemic between the mathematician and astronomer Johannes Kepler (1571-1630) and the esotericist Robert Fludd (1574-1637) concerning the nature of cosmic harmony to argue for a more holistic conception of modern science, one that could include not only the quantitative, scientific approach championed by Kepler but also the qualitative, alchemical approach represented by Fludd (Pauli, 1952, p. 208) In relation to modern science, Pauli stresses above all that in scientific experiments the psyche of the observer has an unavoidable and non-transparent effect on the observations made. Indeed, he argues that "the process of understanding nature [...] seems to be based on a correspondence, a 'matching' of inner images pre-existent in the human psyche with external objects and their behaviour" (1952, p. 152) and he specifically identifies these inner images with archetypes, whose Keplerian and Jungian variants he considers to have "very extensive" agreement (1952, pp. 152-153). For Pauli, the development of scientific ideas "is devoted to adjusting our knowledge to external objects", while inward investigation "should bring to light the archetypal images used in the creation of our scientific concepts" (1952, pp. 208-209). He continues: "Only by combining both these directions of research [the outer, physical and the inner, psychological] may complete understanding be obtained" (1952, p. 209). Importantly, the unavoidable effect of the observer on observations entails for Pauli that there is a relationship between the state of the observer and the knowledge that can be attained – with certain kinds of knowledge therefore requiring a transformation, even a religious transformation, of the observer (1952, p. 212).

"Synchronicity: An Acausal Connecting Principle"

If Pauli's essay argued for the need to take fuller account of the psychic state of the observer when making scientific observations, Jung's essay (CW8, pars. 816-968) advanced a radical proposal as to how the link between observer and observed, between psyche and matter, should be theorised. Jung characterised scientific rationalism – the science which had been ascendant since at least the seventeenth century – as "triadic", based on the three principles of time, space, and causality. His proposal was to introduce synchronicity, or acausal connection through meaning, as a fourth principle (CW8, pars. 961-963; cf. Pauli, 1952, especially pp. 174-175, 204-205, 226-236). This, he argued, would make possible "a whole judgement" (CW8, par. 961) and "a view which includes the psychoid factor [i.e., the archetype understood as psychophysically neutral] in our description and knowledge of nature – that is, an *a priori* meaning or 'equivalence'" (CW8, par. 962).

Exceptional Events

There are at least three important implications of this proposal, each of which contributes to a resolution of some of the problems Jung and Pauli associated with scientific rationalism. First, the fact that meaning is here recognised as a factor able to connect events that would not otherwise be connected allows for the perception of other sets of relationships than causal relationships. Events which might be disregarded from a causal point of view because they are unique, irrational, creative, or outright anomalous – kinds of events important for Jung in fostering individuality – can be grasped from a synchronistic point of view in terms of the patterns of meaning in which they are woven.

Matter imbued with Meaning

Second, Jung's proposal that the archetype is "psychoid" (CW8, pars. 840, 947, 962) and can therefore structure or arrange physical as well as psychic events implies that matter is not, as in the disenchanted worldview fostered by scientific rationalism, fundamentally inert and meaningless – meaning being only something that the human psyche projects onto matter – but rather that matter can be inherently imbued with meaning. Jung states this explicitly to Pauli (7 March 1953): "[I]n cases of synchronicity", he writes, "they [i.e. archetypes] are arrangers of physical circumstances, so that they can also be regarded as a characteristic of Matter (as *the feature that imbues it with meaning*)" (PJL, p. 101; emphasis added). With this claim Jung implies that synchronicity can – at least to some extent (Main, 2011) – reverse the process identified by Max Weber (1864-1920) as "the disenchantment of the world" (1918, p. 155), by Pauli as "the de-animation of the physical world" (1952, p. 156), and by Jung himself as "the historical process of world despiritualization" (CWII, par. 141).

The Spiritualisation of Matter

Third, because the meaning archetypes imbue is for Jung multileveled, ranging from basic levels of ordering, paralleling, and signifying to the kinds of higher levels that inform individual transformation and the framing of meanings of life (Main, 2014), so the meaning in physical circumstances may be complex enough to connect even with religious meanings. This at any rate seems to be implied when Jung, explaining to Pauli his reasons for publishing his religious essay "Answer to Job" (CWII, pars. 553-758) at the same time as his scientific essay on synchronicity, writes that "by making the assumption [in the synchronicity essay] that 'being is endowed with meaning' (i.e., extension of the archetype in the object)" he was attempting "to open up *a new path to the 'state of spiritualization' [Beseeltheit] of Matter*" (PJL, p. 98; emphasis added). The potential implied here for an intimate connection of natural science with not just psychology but also religion opens the prospect for a truly holistic form of understanding.

The Scientific and the Religious for Pauli

These were thoughts to which Pauli, from his very different disciplinary perspective, appears to have been sympathetic. In the letter (27 February 1953) to which Jung's last statement was a response, Pauli had written that he now believed in "the possibility of a simultaneous religious and scientific function of the appearance of archetypal symbols" (PJL, p. 87; cf. Pauli, 1952, p. 212). In a later letter to Jung (23 December 1953) he wrote of his impression that "compensatorily from the unconscious, the tendency is being developed to bring physics much closer to the roots and sources of life, and that what is happening is ultimately *an assimilation of the psychoid archetype into an extended form of physics*" (PJL, p. 130; emphasis added). Later again (23 October 1956), he wrote of certain dreams that seemed to him to be addressing "the problem […] of getting right to the archetypal source of the natural sciences and thus to a new form of religion" (PJL, p. 150).

Integrating the Polemically Excluded: Western Esotericism

It is important to note that the conjunction of science and religion that is envisaged here involves, on the one side, a form of science that engages the symbolic imagination (Pauli, 1952, p. 212) and includes intuition and feeling as well as sensation and thinking (Pauli, 1952, p. 206 and n. 52). On the other side, the form of religion involved is one that privileges relating to the divine through gnosis rather than through faith or reason – "the process of knowing is connected with the religious experience of transmutation undergone by him who acquires knowledge", writes Pauli (1952, p. 212). It is a form of religion in which, in the words of the Egyptologist Jan Assman, "A divine world does not stand in opposition to the world of the cosmos, man, and society; rather it is a principle that permeates it and gives it structure, order, and meaning" (cited in Hanegraaff, 2012, p. 371). As the scholar of Western esotericism Wouter Hanegraaff has argued, these are positions characteristic, if not definitive, of Western esotericism, and as such they have been polemically excluded both by mainstream theistic religions and by mainstream Enlightenment science (2012, pp. 368-379).

Jung described synchronicity as "a modern differentiation of the obsolete concept of correspondence, sympathy, and harmony" (CW8, par. 995), and his list of forerunners of the concept includes several of the most prominent representatives of Western esotericism: Agrippa von Nettesheim, Pico della Mirandola, Paracelsus, and others (CW8, pars. 916-946). At the same time, Pauli chose for his exemplar of a pre-scientific holistic thinker the Paracelsian and Rosicrucian Robert Fludd, and he also seriously entertained the possibility that in the near future "the ancient alchemical idea that matter indicates a psychic state could, on a superior level, experience a new form of realization" (PJL, p. 130). However, Jung's and Pauli's references to "a modern differentiation" and "a superior level" make it clear that they are not recommending a straightforward turn or return to esotericism, but rather are finding something of value in this occulted tradition which can be retrieved and integrated with contemporary physical and psychological knowledge.

Complementarity

What lends promise to this prospective integration where previous attempts at encompassing esotericism within mainstream thought have foundered (Hanegraaff, 2012) is above all the concept of complementarity, whose significance Niels Bohr (1885-1962) had impressed on Pauli (1952, pp. 208-211; see also Pauli, 1950), who in turn influenced Jung's use of it (CW8, pars. 439-440 and n. 130).

Jung did not pit synchronicity, his modern variant of correspondence theory, against causality, or forcibly try to fuse the two principles, but rather presented them as complementary (CW8, pars. 961, 963). Likewise, Pauli did not side with either Kepler's quantitative, scientific approach or Fludd's qualitative, alchemical approach but argued, with explicit reference to complementarity, that "To us, unlike Kepler and Fludd, the only acceptable point of view appears to be one that recognizes *both* sides of reality […] as compatible with each other, and can embrace them simultaneously" (1952, p. 208).

The Cultural Significance of Synchronicity

For Jung and Pauli, the cultural significance of the concept of synchronicity resided first and foremost in the way in which, as Jung wrote to Richard Hull (24 January 1954), it "shakes the security of our scientific foundations" (L2, p. 217) and, as Pauli wrote to Jung (12 December 1950), might provide "a glimpse into the future of natural philosophy" (PJL, p. 65). Yet the particular revision of science towards which synchronicity pointed was one which would integrate it into a bold holistic framework that held together not only such radically diverse kinds of science as physics and psychology but also empirical science as a whole and the trans-empirical field of religion, and not only mainstream science and religion but also some of their occulted countercultural forms.

Acknowledgement

Some of the material in this paper was previously included in R. Main, "Synchronicity and the Problem of Meaning in Science", in H. Atmanspacher and C. Fuchs (eds.) *The Pauli-Jung Conjecture and Its Impact Today*, Exeter: Imprint Academic, 2014.

Bibliography

CW = *The Collected Works of C. G. Jung.* 20 vols. (Sir H. Read, M. Fordham, and G. Adler, Eds.; W. McGuire, Executive Ed.; R. F. C. Hull et al. Trans.). London: Routledge & Kegan Paul, 1953-1973. [Cited by volume and paragraph numbers.]

Gieser, S. (2005). *The Innermost Kernel: Depth Psychology and Quantum Physics – Wolfgang Pauli's Dialogue with C. G. Jung.* Berlin: Springer.

Hanegraaff, W. (2012). *Esotericism and the Academy: Rejected Knowledge in Western Culture.* Cambridge: Cambridge University Press.

Jung, C. G. and Pauli, W (1952). *The Interpretation of Nature and the Psyche* (R. F. C. Hull and P. Silz, Trans.). New York: Pantheon, 1955.

L2 = *C. G. Jung Letters 2: 1951-1961* (Selected and edited by G. Adler in collaboration with A. Jaffé; R. F. C. Hull, Trans.). London: Routledge & Kegan Paul, 1976.

Main, R. (2004). *The Rupture of Time: Synchronicity and Jung's Critique of Modern Western Culture.* Hove and New York: Brunner-Routledge.

Main, R. (2011). "Synchronicity and the Limits of Re-Enchantment", International Journal of Jungian Studies 3:2, 144-158.

Main, R. (2014). "Synchronicity and the Problem of Meaning in Science." In: H. Atmanspacher and C. Fuchs (Eds.), *The Pauli-Jung Conjecture and Its Impact Today.* Exeter: Imprint Academic.

Miller, A. (2009). *Deciphering the Cosmic Number: The Strange Friendship of Wolfgang Pauli and Carl Jung.* New York: Norton.

Pauli, W. (1950). "The Philosophical Significance of the Idea of Complementarity". Chapter in: *Writings on Physics and Philosophy* (C. Enz and K. von Meyenn, Eds.; R. Schlapp, Trans.). Berlin: Springer-Verlag, 1994.

Pauli, W. (1952). "The Influence of Archetypal Ideas on the Scientific Theories of Kepler" (P. Silz, Trans.). In: C. G. Jung and W. Pauli, *The Interpretation of Nature and the Psyche.* New York: Pantheon, 1955.

PJL = *Atom and Archetype: The Pauli/Jung letters 1932-1958* (C. A. Meier, Ed.; D. Roscoe, Trans.). London: Routledge, 2001.

Weber, M. (1918). "Science as a Vocation". In: *From Max Weber: Essays in Sociology* (H. Gerth and C. Wright Mills, Eds. and Trans.). New York: Oxford University Press, 1946.

Friday, 23 August 2013

Introduction

Caterina Vezzoli

Master of Ceremonies

(Italy, CIPA)

Good morning.

It is the last day of our congress and I would like to use the few minutes given to the Masters of Ceremonies to share with you some thoughts on today's theme that can be summarized as: reflections on clinical theory since 1913.

The argumentation concerns Jung's clinical approach and that of Jungians, in response to the changes that have taken place in the real world – in the social sphere, in the sciences, in psychoanalysis. The world context has changed a lot since 1913, the empires, the world equilibriums have changed: two world wars, the end of colonialism, the advent of new forms of economic colonialisms, the crisis of financial capitalism in the West, the concern for the common good represented by the ecological consciousness that could, with difficulty, win over particular interests.

We are not new men or women, but our vision of the world has changed a lot in the last hundred years. Women's education and their entrance into academia with full entitlement, and the social, economic and political world, has contributed to the changes in our societies even though there is still a lot to do. Psychoanalysis and analytical psychology which at first spread in all the western countries then included Eastern Europe and Russia, and now Asia, China, and the Arab world – a challenge in many respects.

This morning's papers will address the study of how the patients' pathologies stimulated the research for the most appropriate clinical approach for that patient with that analyst. Starting first with early Jung, other psychoanalytic theories will be explored and integrated to outline an original Jungian approach "beyond Jung". A clinical thinking that avoids syncretism would exclude the differences instead of including them.

The concern of the papers will be on the therapeutic relationship and on the influence of the analyst in the relationship with the patient. Jung had, since the beginning, questioned the impact of the analyst's personality and theoretical beliefs on the therapy. He also recognized that this influence was not only inevitable but also even necessary for a helpful therapy. With the concepts of participation mystique and countertransference he contributed to the understanding of the influence of the implicit and unconscious elements projected on the analytic relationship. His research on these intuitions had brought him to the point of conceiving the theory of synchronicity and, a hundred years later, at this Congress, we have started to realize their possible effects on our understanding of the world in general and on our clinical practice.

Others after Jung, including many non-Jungians, have studied the concepts of the therapeutic relationship, countertransference and the unconscious influences on the relationship. Their contributions enriched psychoanalysis as well as analytical psychology.

Child analysis is another field that Jungians have cultivated, exploring other theories and at the same time feeling at liberty to integrate them into the Jungian clinical structure. It is possible to move away and explore the progress and the studies of other authors and theorize anew, helped by the opening created by the encounter with the other. Theoretical orthodoxy is not necessary; it is not a value in itself. Clinical and theoretical advances and knowledge are achieved by calling in to discussion what is known.

Jung himself in a letter to Freud on the 3rd of March 1912 wrote: "I would never have sided with you in the first place had not heresy run in my blood". Jung seeks for himself the right and the liberty to explore his interests in his own way. The point might be exactly this: the awareness that there cannot be forbidden frontiers to the analytical investigation; the only limit being the ethical attitude which can be considered a cure in itself, cure of the relationship and of the patient who seeks the help of an analyst. With Jung we have to distinguish between the moral and the ethical: the ethical attitude comes from the unconscious, the moral from conformism. The error, the mortal sin is not the (possible) heresy; it might be a different way of exploring, it is the acceptance of the status quo, of the presumed authority of the known.

Once more, it seems to me that the useful lesson in Jungian analysis is to be a bit of a heretic and even a kind of errant knight constantly searching, ready to question the known. These might be the instruments for working and living creatively our clinical practice and theory.

"Heard with the Eyes": Personal Equation and Fluid Self-State Communication in the Therapeutic Relationship

Cinzia Bressi

(Italy/UK, BJAA)

Dear Colleagues,

Before reading my paper, I would like to introduce myself. My name is Cinzia Bressi and I am a doctor, a professor of psychiatry and psychotherapy at the University of Milan. I am Chair of psychotherapy hospital services at Milan's university hospital where I work, and I also have private practice as a Jungian analyst. I am currently member of the British Jungian Analytic Association, BJAA, one of the four associations of the British Psychotherapy Foundation, of London.

The considerations I shall outline here extend from suggestions in the paper presented by Nadia Fina, which I found extremely interesting and rich in content. In the wake of these considerations, I would like to begin by asking a question: how does the analyst's personal equation "act" in the transference/countertransference dynamics that develop in the analytic relationship?

Jung saw the analyst's personal equation as being subjective prejudice that risked not being subjected to transformative criticism (CW16). On this basis, he postulated types of personal equation that are based on the predominance of one function of conscious orientation or the other.

But what did Jung understand by "subjective prejudice"? He maintained that it was a product of an individual's accumulated self-experience, which could be refined to a greater or lesser extent. It was an encounter, or better still, Jung (ibid.) described the personal equation in psychotherapeutic practice as a collision between an individual mind and environmental conditions, thus representing a subjective edition of general experience.

The encounter between an individual and his self-experience makes him unique, but also subject to acting according to his subjective prejudice when interacting with another individual. Out of this derives the need to observe both oneself and the world, the relationship both with one's own inner experience and that of the other, after having worked on the self at length and on the development of subjectivizing and individuative thought.

Jung wrote that a therapist could be totally unable to perceive in a patient what he did not see in himself, or alternatively, that his perceptions could be amplified, thus either encouraging the patient towards objectives that are actually his own or else condemning the patient for what he rejected about himself (CW16).

It was Jung, once again, who observed that each therapy was a single "dialectic process" in which the analyst as a person was involved just as much as the patient. And, if the analyst feels a hit or is tripped up by the patient, it need not be a bad thing, as he can heal to the extent that he himself has been injured – and here we can recall the mythologem of the "Wounded Healer".

As I was writing these lines, it came to mind that in the Adult Attachment Interview by Mary Main, R. Goldwin and Erik Hesse (2003), which I frequently use given that I work with adolescents and their parents, there are several questions that are extremely important when assessing what the wounded child did during his childhood, who he sought out and how he behaved when he was emotionally or physically hurt or ill. "What would usually happen?" "How did you react to the pain?" "And your parents, how did they respond?"

This helps us to observe what today's adults, who are unable to "maintain" a relationship with their adolescent child, were like as children: they would shut themselves in their bedrooms and put a sticking plaster on by themselves, thus "protecting" themselves twice over, by going somewhere they held was safe and by providing their wounds with "protection", crying alone, not asking anyone for help, except, perhaps, their brothers or sisters, on occasion.

It is during the times of physical or mental pain that a child seeks his/her attachment figures, a parent who ought to nurse, care for and "hold" the child. These experiences, which are essential to strengthening, developing and giving direction to the child's nuclear Self, call for support, closeness, comfort and help from attachment figures.

The experiences that belong to today's mothers and fathers were, and still are, being dismissed and excluded. Or rather, these children, who are now parents, would look to *their* parents for some concrete care, a bandage, or hospital, and would then idealize help and salvific treatments, which perpetuates the sustenance only of the split-off parts of the Self, the parts that could not be penetrated by thought. States of mind which distance pain through dismissiveness, or states of mind that were witness to these individuals' anger and confusion, or even to their being overwhelmed at times by traumas and their own parents' shortcomings, were thus confirmed, rendering adequate parenting less achievable. In response to the question: "In your opinion, why did your parents behave as they did during your childhood?" the answers are banal, *jargon, psychobabble, or canned statements,* as they have come to be known.

For some time now, I have been reflecting upon the extent to which patients' attachment styles and mental states are at the core of their projective identifications, and the extent to which an analyst's responses featuring projective counteridentifications depend on his/hers attachment style.

Fordham considered countertransference as projective identification that was a useful source of information about the patient's state of mind if the analyst accepted that he "might find himself behaving in ways that were out of line with what he knew of himself, but syntonic with what he knew of his patient" (1996:165). He then went on to explain that "the whole analytic situation is a mass of illusions, delusions, displacements, projections and introjections" (1996:172, also referred to by J. Knox, 2011).

As observed by Jung and developed by contemporary psychoanalytic thought, the analytic process features verbal actions, non-verbal actions and interactions. Levenson (1983) places *the language of speech and the language of action* together, to the point that one is a transformation of the other. So the analyst's inevitable continuous participation is thus further confirmed. And we are already aware that the observer is inevitably part of what is observed.

For example, Levine (1994) has pointed out that the analyst's interpretations always hold some performance or action-like qualities, in that the analyst's words are a kind of an unintentional action. I would like to highlight this, as enactment belongs to the analyst's subjective responses that are intrinsically related to his or her psychology, which, as I stress, is *not personalistic* but personal. And, dynamic interaction processes of destruction and reparation in the analytic relationship are the result of the analyst's, as well as the patient's, active unconscious contribution (Beebe & Lachmann, 2002).

We know that the analyst's reflective or mentalization function is compromised during mutual enactments. As Donnel B. Stern (2008) has observed, when the analyst is blindly involved in the relationship with the patient because of an unconscious motivation, he can mentalize neither his own experience nor that of the patient. In such situations, I believe that in addition to the analyst's personal equation, the timing of the reflective mental space, where the analyst can "hold" the content of the reflective identification, that is, a dissociated and non-representable part of the patient's mind, is also of extreme importance.

During an enactment, if the analyst reacts directly to the patient's projective identification, the belief that the inner and outer worlds are the same is consolidated (psychic equivalence). But if the analyst accepts the patient's projective identification, and is not immediately provoked into reacting to it, as has already been pointed out by Nadia Fina using different words, and if this experience can be transformed, mentalized and given back to the patient, then enactment will not occur. The analysand can then begin to take his or her first steps away from psychic equivalence and towards the first signs of reflective functioning. And the sensitivity and empathy coming from the analyst, when shared meaning is being constructed with the patient. will boost the therapeutic alliance.

Since enactments are the only form of representable dissociated material, they are, nevertheless, a tremendous source of information about the patient. I therefore agree with Donnel Stern that understanding and insight are not essential when responding to projective identification. In order to grasp and accommodate the inedited, split off and unthought aspects of the patient's experience that he/she is totally unable to express in words, working solidly on the unconscious influence that the patient has on the analyst and the crisis the patient has provoked is indeed preferable. Much of this experience is not verbalized, it is dissociated and it is laden with affect.

Jean Knox has extended this idea with her suggestion of "developmental attunement" (Knox, 2011:166), which requires the analyst to use his or her own countertransference reactions to identify the specific nature and developmental content that was inhibited during the patient's development and used in the projective identification. From countless studies, we are aware that non-verbal affective transactions, such as the analyst's facial expressions, posture, movement, and emotional tone of voice, play a fundamental role in unconscious emotional interactions. According to Schore, these "co-create an intersubjective context that allows for the structural expansion of the patient's orbitofrontal system and its cortical and subcortical connection" (2003: 264).

This observation takes us back to attachment theory, which claims that the infant does not interiorize the object but the specific relational dynamics between the Self and the other (Beebe & Lachmann, 2002).

In order to modulate affect regulation, the analyst's tone of voice, body language, facial expressions and gestures are all extremely important. As opposed to causing the analyst's reflective function to collapse, projective counteridentification can be used effectively as containment right from the look in the analyst's eyes, before he/she even utters a word, and then from their tone of voice: in essence, from everything the *analyst is*. The personal equation thus becomes not just an encounter between the Self and life experience (as Jung puts it), but also the ability to *be with* the patient regardless of aggressive content, fear or terror with no name that the analysand may have transferred into the analyst's Self. Negotiation between isolated subjectivities can thus take place and gradually begin to replace the patient's dissociative shell (Bromberg, 2008). Conditions can thus be created so that the little girl who has violently knocked her head against the glass table in the living room, recognizing only the blood that is gushing out of the deep wound on her temple, will not, while crying and terrified, go to seek "protection" in her bedroom, but will be able to obtain "recognition". According to Ronald Laing (1962), confirmation of our identity does not depend so much on others' approval but on others' *recognition*, that is, on the accurate perception they bear of the way in which we experience ourselves (Bromberg, 2008).

As analysts, if we receive our analysand's pain and terror without reacting or without seeking to change them, then these islands of affective reality, these parts of the Self that were initially dissociated, can be recognized, perceived and guided towards self-reflection through symbolic ability and verbal forms that are expressed within a relational context.

When one of my analysands, as I was showing him into my consulting room just a few minutes after the scheduled time of our session, said: "I thought you had forgotten about me"; or when another, after one of her sessions had been rescheduled, became visibly agitated and said in a disturbed voice, "so it's true that you are leaving ... and what about me ... ?", I cannot but think, given that I know their life stories, about the extent to which a developmental trauma is still active in their lives as it is in the *here and now* of our relationship.

During the early stages of life, if some parts of the Self are systematically disavowed, *then continuing to exist in another's mind – and therefore in one's own eyes – like the child Self in front of his parents*, is a lot more difficult. In order to achieve its top priority of maintaining stability, the nuclear Self, which underpins procedural memory, will continue to employ early models of attachment based on how much it saw reflected in the mother's eyes. If, however, the parents denied the relational existence of several aspects of the nuclear Self, then these are what will make up the core of the projective identification.

I believe that in the analyst's personal equation, the development of his own nuclear Self, that is, when the analyst was "his parents' child", cannot be overlooked. This image generally continues to evolve throughout life though reshaping itself so that the Self can change and become integrated into an individual pattern, which, for the most part, is not dissociated.

It is for this reason that the pain and terror passed on to the analyst's Self by the patient needs to create the real danger of the person's destruction. The analyst must leave some time and mental space where these terrifying conditions will not be modified, and ask himself, also according to what he can see in his patient's eyes – a child in front of his parents – what are these dissociated parts that are asking to be born *out of and in the relationship*.

For this reason, the communication between the analyst and the analysand cannot be fluid at the start of the analytic journey. Each will be isolated, even within the relationship, and this will lead to repeated collisions between the patient's and the analyst's subjectivity. This repetition itself means that a relational process will be generated out of these collisions, where the "new" will create a space between the two players. Bromberg referred to these collisions as "safe surprises", since the new that emerges in projective identification, projective counteridentification and enactments, is the result of "the fear circuitry" being activated in *not-too-safe* conditions, according to LeDoux (1996). Under these conditions, the failures of the past are repeated in the analytic relationship with "something extra" that belongs to the patient's developmental drive. And it is out of these emotional storms that the analyst's Self has taken upon it, that the *new* can suddenly emerge. And using Jung's words, the new will emerge in the therapeutic relationship out of the old that has been either dismantled or surmounted.

The heart of these analytical aspects is the dynamic relationship that Jung called the transcendent function, where the "union of conscious and unconscious is consummated" (Jung, CW9). In other words, the transcendent function can be interpreted as a constant, dynamic confrontation and "integration of explicit conscious information and memories with the more generalized knowledge that we accumulate uncounsciously in the internal working models of implicit memory, a key part of which constitutes the sense of Self" (Knox, 2011, p.179). This process attributes meaning and significance to inner experience as well as to relational experience, which will then go on to contribute to the patient's process of individuation.

Until the individual shall authentically and entirely perceive him/herself in the eyes of the other.

Bibliography

Beebe, B., Lachmann, F. (2002) Infant research and adult treatment: Co-constructing interactions. Hillsdale NJ: Analytic Press.

Bromberg, P.M. (2008) *"Mentalize this"* Dissociation, *Enactment, and Clinical process*. In Mind to Mind. Infant research, neuroscience, and psychoanalysis (E.L. Jurist, A. Slade, S. Bergner, Editors). New York: Other Press.

Fordham, M. (1996) Analytical psychology and countertransference. In S. Shamsadami (Ed.) Analyst-patient interaction: Collected papers on technique (Chapter 15), London: Routledge.

Jung, C.G. (1966) *General problems of psychotherapy. Fundamental questions of psychotherapy.* In: Collected Works of C. G. Jung: Vol. 16. (G. Adler & R.F.C. Hull, Ed and Trans). Princeton, NJ: Princeton University Press.

Jung, C.G. (1969) *Conscious, unconscious and individuation.* In: Collected Works of C. G. Jung: Vol. 9, part 1 (G. Adler & R.F.C. Hull, Ed and Trans). Princeton, NJ: Princeton University Press.

Knox, J. (2011) Self-agency in psychotherapy: attachment, autonomy and intimacy. New York: W W Norton & Company.

Laing, R.D. (1962) *Confirmation and disconfirmation*. In The Self and others. Chicago: Quadrangle books.

LeDoux, J.E. (1996) *The emotional brain*. New York: Touchstone.

Levenson, E.A. (1983) *The ambiguity of change*. New York: Basic

Levine, H.B. (1994) "The analyst's participation in the analytic process" *International Journal of psychoanalysis*. 75, 665-676.

Main, M., Goldwin, R., Hesse, E. (2003) *Adult Attachment Scoring and Classification System*. Unpuplished manuscript. University of California, Berkeley.

Stern, D.B. (2008) *On having to find what you don't know how to look for*. In Mind to Mind. Infant research, neuroscience, and psychoanalysis (E.L. Jurist, A. Slade, S. Bergner, Editors). New York: Other Press

Countertransference and Projective Counteridentification

Nadia Fina

(Italy, AGAP)

All psychoanalysts, regardless of their theoretical background, fully agree that the transference and countertransference are correlated and indispensable to therapeutic work.

Alongside these "mechanisms" which underpin the analytic process is that of projective counteridentification. It was Grinberg in 1957 who put forward the concept of projective counteridentification as a mechanism that describes a particular expressive feature of the countertransference. He saw it as the expression of the therapist's particularly intense experiences, which emerge from a certain kind of weave: one made up of both the content and the psychopathological manner in which projective identification is used by the patient, arousing extremely particular states of mind as well as anxious and emotional responses in the therapist, which lead to his or her making reactive interpretations and comments. Due to the sheer volume of identifications and projections, various different roles and fantasies belonging to the patient are 'interpreted' by the analyst *'passively'* or unconsciously.

Undoubtedly, in Grinberg's view, the countertransference is mainly the patient's *creation*, the patient's *product*. However, this way of thinking bears heavy foreclosure. Jung had instead considered such as the basis of the entire therapeutic process: or rather, he placed the personal equation in this light, it being that specific quality of the analytical dyad's subjectivities, which enter into mutual, dialectic play.

Returning to Grinberg and his line of thought, he saw the severity of the patient's psycho-pathological condition as determining the quality and quantity of the therapist's counterprojective responses. That said, he clearly saw projective identification as necessary since it brings about the empathic relationship that enables the analyst to put him- or herself in the patient's shoes. He recognised how important this was, seeing it as a characteristic of the subjective mind and the basis of human communication. In fact, he underlined that the object empathy it is directed towards has its projective identifications too, without which there would be no mutual exchange.

And it is this very form of communication which plays a crucial role in the symbolic formation of the mind. But, the extent to which projective identifications are 'normal', according to Grinberg, depends on the nature of the projective identifications that are at work in the patient's primary object relations. And the therapist's counteridentificatory response will be more 'neurotic' the narrower his or her awareness is of being a 'victim of one's own unresolved and unhealthy experiences, which ought to be *eliminated*' (Sic!)

I believe that the underlying idea of Grinberg's analysis of counteridentification is essentially one that is too firmly anchored to the mechanism as well as to the drive as the predominant cause, and within which the therapist's sanity is equivalent to the excision of each and every emotional part. It thus loses sight of the fact that an individual's emotions, feelings and thoughts –and the analyst is an individual– are expressions of joy and pain, of problems and their possible solution. It loses sight of the fact that ambivalence and transformation are experiences that accompany each of us along our journey through life and that the point an analyst should reach is awareness of the negative, and being able to manage and use the negative in the best ways possible. The idea that the analyst has been purified of the negative is a dangerous ideological grounding that is dehumanizing and which nudges the analyst towards inflated omnipotence.

Projective counteridentification should instead be reconsidered not as an expression of the analyst's neurotic disorder, but as a potential skill, the heightened awareness of which can activate the pre-conscious empathically towards who the patient is and what he or she wants us to feel: raw experiences that cannot be put into words since they are not thinkable; implicit relational communication that finds room for expression through archaic means, which does not make them any less important as signals of something that needs to be understood; experiences that certainly indicate the patient's deep and often severe mental distress.

An analyst who understands the profound importance of the personal equation as an expression of the analytic relationship, can, for instance, sense his or her patient's depressive identification, but without actually becoming depressed, insofar as his or her permeability is elastic but elective at the same time. As well as being a container, the analyst must also think of him- or herself as a *filter*, capable of establishing *the right distance of pathos*. This is a particular modulating skill that concerns the analyst's unconscious contents just as much as it does the patient, the aim of which is to avoid being caught up in extreme oscillations: that is, those that go from massive identification to icy, freezing disidentification.

If the concept of counteridentification is taken to the extreme and ideologized, thus drifting from the very nature of the relational exchange, it then becomes highly defensive for the analyst. Attributing the responsibility of the countertransference to the patient is, after all, a way of distancing the analyst's emotional participation from the relationship with the patient. Searls, for instance, conceptualizes a mechanism which is the exact opposite of this. He repeatedly points out that it is the psychoanalyst's unconscious which is "responsible" for bringing about projective counteridentification phenomena *in the patient*, to the extent that he or she is driven towards instances of acting out.

Within the Jungian model, the analyst enters into the analytical relationship right from the very beginning with all his or her meaning and essence, with all his or her emotional, mental and formal potential. The analyst's most difficult task is that of guiding the other individual towards his or her subjectivation or individuation. It is both clear and understandable that, within this model, each outbreak of idio-syncrasies, projective and introjective emotional compulsions and/or personalistic ideologies, disintegrates the therapist's subjective quality and seriously interferes with the analyst-patient relationship. Such could be defined as personal immaturity that clouds over meaning.

Everything the analyst says and does in analysis is personal, *extremely personal*. The countertransference becomes neurotic when it degen-erates from personal to personalistic, that is, when the relational tension drops and the analyst *reacts* as opposed to *acting or not acting*. And by "acting or not acting", I am referring to the ability to contain one's own and the patient's emotions, so as to keep the interpersonal relationship free and unburdened.

Within this field of transference / countertransference dynamics, the "personal or real" relationship manifests something of its own, which can be defined according to the Jungian theoretical model. Transference / countertransference dynamics is what the therapeutic alliance rests on, and the analyst cannot but be an object of the patient's investments and projections. This simple statement places before us the idea that the analyst can be an **object** *invested by a projection* or *a* **subject** *who receives a projection*. In the first case – an *object* invested by a projection – our reference is taken from a theory of the mind that is still anchored to the drive dimension, since the patient's object-relations representations are considered mainly as being the result of aggressive drives, of the patient's self representa-tions which move within a field of object relations drive transference. In the second case – a **subject** who receives a projection – we find ourselves instead within a theoretical dimension that explains the projective transference area itself as an expression of an affective dimension that is the **result** of distortions and/or deviations that have arisen out of deficiencies in the patient's exchange with his or her significant objects.

This difference is important, as it underpins the idea that the therapist is experienced *also* as a real person as opposed to predominantly being a build-up of projections. Before the contents of the patient's psychic world, the analyst displays a certain degree of solidity and substance, which first and foremost enables him or her to be included in the analysand's inner world. This experience subsequently shifts towards the world of outer reality. The analyst thus helps the patient to *bind* a stable enough composition of self-representations in '**relation-with**', thanks also to a stabilizing perceptive experience. The form the bond takes is modulated by regulating and transforming the relationship with an actual selfobject/analyst.

Clearly, this does not mean that the analyst is not, time and again during an analysis, also a 'site' where projections are placed. We are well aware that there are patients who really put the analyst's ability to maintain containment to the test, and can arouse or cause neurotic or personalistic countertransference reactions. But an analyst who does not forget that he or she is a real person can develop and maintain optimal tension, enabling him or her to make important interpretations at the right moment and in the most appropriate way so that they may be accepted and understood empathically by the patient.

The analyst above all needs to understand that an objective, static, unbending truth does not exist, since each truth is one that is intra- and inter-personal within the relational *hic et nunc*. The relationship with the analyst thus becomes a cohesive or integrative experience for the two psychic dimensions that weigh down the patient's personality: conflict and deficit.

This integration, on which affective and psychological health depends, is needed today more than ever, considering the patterns of symptoms and severe pathologies that patients who come to our practices have: pathologies that derive from early and pervasive deficits that have formed amassed, trauma-like structures, thus hampering the construction of an affective and mental apparatus.

At the same time, contemporary psychoanalysis focuses – in the area of the transference – on offering an experience that is **appropriate to the patient's current circumstances**, one which structurally corresponds to the selfobject, an object that can activate and promote development, and which should have been found by the analysand during childhood in the maternal "environment". And it is this new object-relations experience that brings about profound transformation, thanks to the analyst being experienced by the patient as an individual who is able to "authentically" approach his or her suffering.

Within the notion of the countertransference that includes projective counteridentification as a form of authentic experience that the analyst needs to become aware of patients' acting-in and -out may be reconsidered as an attempt, a repetitive attempt, at provoking and pushing the analyst's "neutral" position towards breaking point; an attempt at putting the analyst to the test in order to obtain his or her emotional participation in the analytic relationship, participation which, in the long term, can heighten the analyst's awareness and therefore increase the potential of the analytic couple.

Countertransference and projective counteridentification need to be verified according to the form and content of the material the patient produces, and to the interaction of the analytic couple, so that what it is in the patient that causes the therapist's responses and how such come about can be clearly understood. The analyst needs to explore how the patient stimulates his or her countertransference responses and what this means for them both.

This is because we must never forget that mental illness hinders development and the ability to change, but it is nevertheless the subject's often necessary product, one which contains not only pain and suffering but also a request for freedom and for an endless number of hidden meanings to be understood. Nor should we lose sight of the fact that the *theory used* can also influence the analyst's countertransference and impair clinical judgment.

Searls, back in the late 1960s, with ideas that came out of his research on projective activity with psychotic patients, and which surprisingly converged with Jung's thought, underlined that even the therapist is not exempt from investing the analysand with projections. Being unaware of these emotional movements in the relationship certainly contributes to bringing about projective counteridentification, but *the patient's*, and for this reason he or she can do nothing but act out and the like. The therapist's awareness must be directed towards the external and the internal simultaneously so as to perceive the patient's splitting.

If it were really the case that the analyst's projective counteridentification is mainly the patient's creation, it stirring up unresolved neurotic areas in the analyst, then we would run the serious risk of thinking that the patient is *always* psychotic and that the analyst is always right, no matter what he or she says – even the most absurd and intellectualistic interpretation – as long as it is justified by theory. All of the analyst's maturity, all of his or her effort to reach an adequate level of awareness must be used to discriminate between how much is projection, that is, the patient's activity, and how much is owing to his or her own hypersensitivity, susceptibility and emotional and ideological reactions. The therapist is thus in a position to either exalt or dampen the patient's projective counteridentification.

Projective identification and projective counteridentification impact on both holding and containment, which are active in the therapeutic process: As suggested by Ogden, **holding** in the strict sense of the term, which concerns the ontological level and the establishment of a sense of temporal continuity; and **containment** that instead concerns the creation of an apparatus which is able to transform sensory and affective perceptions into thinkable thoughts, and, through the setting, is transformed into awareness of movement between break and empathy –that is, attention on the part of the analyst towards the steady rhythm of the patient's unfolding.

Moments of Embodiment

Judith Woodhead
(UK, SAP)

I begin with words from T.S. Eliot's "Four Quartets":

> Time present and time past
> Are both perhaps present in time future,
> And time future contained in time past.

My presentation is about moments, moments and embodiment, moments of embodiment.

After initial thoughts about the words, followed by a sequence of images, I shall illustrate present moments of clinical work with an adult patient in analysis. Turning to infancy, we will then see a DVD clip of a robust baby, during nappy change time, followed by a clip of embodied communication between an infant and his grandfather. I will then show three DVD sequences of moments that arise between an infant, mother, father and therapist in parent-infant psychotherapy.

Embodiment suggests an idea, quality, or feeling. The IAAP, for example, *embodies* Jungian analysis worldwide. The structure and sound of the word em-body-ment suggests "in-body-state," a feeling of existing and living in physical being. It is a linguistic evocation of a relationship between body and mind, a subjective mental-emotional-body-soul qualitative feeling, a state of being" meaning "to move" suggests shifting time. Moments of embodiment evoke nuggets of time in which we feel solid, housed, embedded in being, inside rather than outside of one-self. The opposite are moments of feeling scattered, fragmented, broken up, in parts, or bits, "dis-embodied." Feelings of embodiment can be regarded as images, that "need not be pictorial but can manifest kinesthetically" Evetts-Secker (2012). Embodiment in Donald Winnicott's words (1958), is a process of "personalization", suggestive of becoming, a "psychosomatic unity," evocative of a togetherness state, an "in-dwelling." Yet, this word "embodiment", like the experience of embodied moments, is mercurial, slippery, difficult to catch hold of and have firm meaning. T.S. Eliot suggests:

> Words strain,
> Crack and sometimes break, under the burden,
> Under the tension, slip, slide, perish,

Decay with imprecision, will not stay in place,
Will not stay still. Shrieking voices
Scolding, mocking, or merely chattering,
  Always assail them.

There now follows a sequence of images, of ancient and contemporary times, to enliven our minds and add texture to thought.

We move now to my patient, Janet, in her late sixties, four years into her analysis, who told me one day of a feeling of "being dragged" to the date of a hospital operation, a month away. She felt hurried inexorably to that specific moment, with so many tasks to be done, and not enough time. I spoke of how it was as if time was pulling her, a kind of mental feeling of going fast. We thought of her manic episodes, when she would be up, active in the night because, she suggested "it was better than lying alone unable to go to sleep." Exploring those moments she reflected, "It is so frightening to stay in the present, better to distract myself by doing." We spoke of childhood times when she never knew, from one moment to the next, whether her mother's mental and emotional states would frighten and overwhelm her. She would keep quiet, go to bed and listen, fearful, to violent episodes downstairs, sounds of loud voices and kitchen objects breaking. I said, "So frightened about what might happen next." She replied, "I would feel un-held." We spoke how present moments were indeed to be feared. We recalled her mother coming while Janet sat on the outside toilet, threateningly brandishing a big kitchen knife at her. There was quiet. I spoke of the solidity of the couch beneath her, just now. After some time, she said the word that had formed in the quietness of her mind, from nowhere, was 'un-hinged.' Together we amplified the image of the hinge that holds things together. Janet suggested, "I like a box when the lid opens, but if the hinge comes off then it becomes unhinged, like my mother was." She expressed her deepest fear not to become like her. The hinges were, she said, important to keep her safe. There was quiet. I remarked with feeling in my words, "And your poor old body, with all its pains." She responded, "My body just has to get on with it, do as it is told. The fastness in my mind stops me being in my body." A shift occurred to a feeling of profound stillness, of the slow passage of time, of co-creation of co-being, in the present moment. She eventually remarked that just now she was feeling the present moments, both her mind and her body together. I said, "And the breath that comes and goes, and the beating of the quiet heart." As our time ended, she (and I a little) stretched. I said, "Gently, gently and slowly, no rush," as she climbed down stiffly from the couch, her joints so painful. The intersubjective matrix had shifted.

I felt in those moments that we were "alive and conscious, only now. Now is when we actively feel to be in our own lives, and when we directly live our lives. Everything else is once or twice removed. The only time of raw subjective reality, of phenomenal experience, is the present moment" (Stern 2004). A mind-psyche, in the absence of emotional care, takes over to organise the caring for psyche-soma. It becomes "extra active, on guard, as if outside of the body, a dis-location between psyche and soma – the mind localised in the head" (Winnicott, 1949). A self-care system develops "that preserves the spark of each person's divine inheritance – the innocent soul – but at the price of its disembodiment and de-animation" (Kalsched 2013).

"People change, and smile: but the agony abides" wrote T. S. Eliot. Dis-embodiment, de-animation evokes di-ssociative strategies for defence against the ravages of trauma and pain. Jung wrote: "The emotional significance of the experience remains hidden all along from the patient so that, not reaching consciousness, the emotion never wears itself out, it is never used up." A shadow casts itself forwards over the span of emotional and bodily life. For Janet and many of my adult patients, the analytic frame and the quality of the symbolic couch, embodies solidness, space and time needed for undoing the tyranny of the traumatised mind over the body, so new present moments can come into being and re-shape past present moments. When the present moment can be fully lived a qualitative coming together of different parts of the self emerges, an integration, a feeling of wholeness, "quick now, here, now, always" (T.S. Eliot).

Before we move on to explore the therapy sequences, we are going to look through the lens of our embodiment theme at a clip of a robust baby with his mother in an ordinary family setting. It opens with baby James, his parents' third child, crying while his mummy changes his nappy. The household bustles with ordinary, lively family life, brothers' voices in the background of the DVD clip. Mother cleans her baby boy, oils his body, talking with my colleague videoing them, about forthcoming circumcision, saying to her baby "You don't look forward to that." She tells him, rather indirectly while attending to the physical tasks: "You get into such a state." He continues crying. His mummy takes her time throughout the process before lifting her loudly vociferating baby to face her, saying: "You get yourself in such a state, don't you? You get yourself in such a state." With these present affect-laden words, he quietens and they look deeply into each other. "Where are your tears?" says his mummy. She talks to him about changing him, about the oil now getting onto her clothes. "Oh, but mummy you're lovely, you're lovely mummy" says my colleague behind the video camera Mother and baby become immersed in one another. The DVD clip of James and his other was shown in the presentation.

James could communicate feeling and need that (eventually) shifted from one moment to the next, as he and his mother came together in real alive present moments. We saw the change from communication through whole body protest to a mutually regulated moment of attunement, an integrated whole body-soul experience, shifting from movement to focused stillness. In Eliot's poetic language:

> At the still point of the turning world. Neither flesh, nor fleshless;
> Neither from, nor towards; at the still point, there the dance is,
> But neither arrest, nor movement. And do not call it fixity.
> Where past and future are gathered. Neither movement from nor towards,
> Neither ascent nor decline. Except for the point, the still point,
> There would be no dance, and there is only the dance.

We are now going to see a relational dance that arises between seven-week-old Jordan and his grandfather. Eyes and mouths mirror one another, as Jordan's whole body moves. It is a wonderful evocation of Daniel Stern's (1985) "vitality affects" that involve intense dynamic shifts or patterned change. Also experiencing slippage of words and meanings, Stern (2010) expanded the phrase to become "dynamic forms of vitality" that have intensity, force, movement, space and directionality of time. The Johnson and Johnson's DVD clip of Jordan and grandfather were shown in the presentation.

Infants risk lacking dynamic forms of vitality when their family system cannot embody them. The James sequence, the Jordan and grandfather interactions, are lively present moments of vital embodied relating. Such "now moments" arise at moments of affective intensity, strong feeling, that change relating. They are qualitatively different, unexpected moments of present significance, with a kairos quality. When a "now moment" is contingently responded to, and a "moment of meeting" occurs, the infant's activity and state changes and a new qualitatively different feeling of relationality occurs. Such shifting moments shape a new open space and a new equilibrium. In the words of the Quartets:

> Time past and time future
> What might have been and what has been
> Point to one end, which is always present.

I am going to describe and then show the three sequences of moments in my work as Jungian parent-infant psychotherapist in which a relational dance begins to unfold. Parent-infant psychotherapy, an innovative expansion of psychoanalytic technique, provides an intersubjective matrix of infant-oriented time and space, in which the baby can initiate and respond to relational actions. Therapeutic work, during the formation of the infant's implicit memory, requires focus on the present in a Winnicottian "facilitating environment" in which the infant can initiate action and states of being with an-other and experience attuned responses. The baby's personality, temperament, whole psyche, connection with ancestors, culture and potential futures are present. As the fetus is womb-embedded, so the infant needs to become mind-embodied. The work comprises critical present moments because the baby's developmental agenda cannot wait. The therapy interrupts an infant's composition of intrapsychic theatre scripts that may surface in later life as psychosomatic states, emotional illness or not being able to experience and know what we feel.

The work combines reflective and verbal activity in the therapist, in relation with the pre-verbal infant and verbal parents. The Boston Change Process Study Group, whose work is implicit in this paper (along with the work of Joseph Cambray and George Hogenson on emergence, synchronicity and dynamic systems) show how 'the implicit and reflective-verbal domains share a similar microstructure, of the micro-unit that underlies subjective experience in the "present moment" (BCPSG, 2008). It is, they suggest, intentions, experienced through mirror neurons, that organize such 'now moments', embodied in "a lived story with a narrative like format that is grasped intuitively while it is unfolding." In a baby's early life the experience of relationally embodied creative narrative is crucial. 'Words are not discarnated symbols but are also pathways into direct embodied experience'.

The moments I shall now describe and show are from sequences from the first, second and fourth sessions of work with the baby, mother and father. Each of the three sequences is entitled with words the mother used: *"I don't think he knows I'm his mum," "Very in love with him"* and *"I've never seen him this vocal before."* I will show the DVD clips after reading the sequences, with thoughts about meanings, so that our active imaginations can bring the work alive, and help us to absorb as much as can when we see the clips.

The infant was in deep relational difficulty when I first met him. Born by C-Section at near full term, he weighed only seven pounds (three kg.) at six weeks old, when the therapy began. The psychiatric department of the local hospital where the baby was born, had first seen the mother when thirty-two weeks pregnant, due to her hyperemesis gravidarum. She vomited so continually during the whole pregnancy that she was hospitalised, including for the last two months. Her psychiatrist referred her to a specialist counselor in the hospital who, due to worry about the mother's non-engagement with her baby, referred the family to our Centre. Given the urgency of this case, I offered the family an appointment within a week. Babies cannot wait.

The first sequence: the baby is six weeks old (DVD clip)

"I Don't Think He Knows I'm His Mum."

The mother's feeling of not knowing she was her baby's mother framed the first session. The session began before it's beginning. The infant's screams filled the Anna Freud Centre for twenty minutes (they had arrived early to try to bottle feed him his Formula) before their session was due to begin. This baby cried so loudly his voice had become literally hoarse; he had little voice left. His cries deeply penetrated and alarmed me while doing administration in a distant room. No longer able to bear the baby's states, I arrived early in the waiting room. I found the infant's father holding such a tiny baby; he said he did not know what to do with him. His wife told me she could hold him only for a very short time once a day; she said with dread in her voice that she could not carry him to the therapy room. Her fear was palpable; her face set in a fixed, depressed expression, her voice lifeless, disconnected. The family's unfolding narrative about their situation catalysed me to enter into their family system. Individuation processes sparked. It is often said that Jung viewed individuation as from mid-life onwards. Parent-infant work has crystallized my view of an infant as a whole psyche, already a little "individuator" teleogically weaving his or her life out of early personal, family, cultural and historical experience.

Father carried his baby to the therapy room, upright on his shoulder, his tiny body stiff, his expression suggesting a dissociated state, the beginnings of "an adaptive defensive structure, developed to protect the nascent or traumatised self" (Wilkinson, 2010). His father, suffering from back pain, sat on a chair holding his son, while mother and I sat on floor-cushions. Father, exhausted, unfolded their shared story. His wife could not participate in their baby's care. Maternal grandmother helped him provide all the care in their home. The baby's mother could not be with him. She would watch him from a distance, not able to move closer. She never fed him. She slept in a separate room, while her husband looked after their baby son in the parental bedroom. Father then spoke affectionately of his baby, spoke softly to him, and expressed his longing for his wife and baby to get to know one another.

Dis-connection between mother and son was acute. There was no erotic current, an absence of movement between them, no looking, no forward gestures towards one another, a stiff, static, detached maternal stance of recoil. In the womb, intense vomiting periods meant she could keep nothing inside her, apart from the baby. She, and her growing baby within, was in hospital including for the last two months of pregnancy. An Anna Freud Centre Bulletin paper (1982) suggests the baby's experience in utero of the vomiting rhythms evokes an image of "a baby whose brain or mind became patterned to a diaphragm that was constantly doing a rumba (dance)" who may expect that life outside the womb will be the same as his mind had become accustomed to inside. Thus the baby's crying activity, with all its bodily impact, could be a reflection of his experience in utero. Feelings of "primary maternal persecution" (Raphael-Leff, 1996) needed help to turn into "primary maternal preoccupation" (Winnicott). Perhaps the mother needed physical separation to ensure emotional detachment rather than attachment to a baby embedded within her body. The life-shifting momentous events of pregnancy and birth can awaken complexes. Perhaps she felt she needed to protect the baby from her difficult, painful feelings. If we imagine now ourselves in the baby's position, we would feel we have a mother who is emotionally and physically unavailable, disengaged. What can the baby do? If he seeks to identify and relate with mother, the positive affect accompanying this urge to find his mother's face and become beheld would fall, resulting in Stern's "micro-depressions", the result of repeated emergent moments that meet a lack of response. One solution is for a baby to fill the relational gap with his own psyche-soma as substitute for mother.

The biographical narrative continued. I learnt the baby spent eight days in neonatal care, his mother saddened that she couldn't see him until the second day. Their situation felt so hopeless that, twenty minutes into this first meeting, I asked if they would like me to hold their baby. Relieved, they agreed and father placed him into my arms.

Sitting close with mother, I held the baby facing over my shoulder, close to my body, voicing their trauma. The baby felt stiff and un-moulding, un-embedding in my arms. Holding him brought direct bodily communication of the baby's needs for embodiment. It gave him contact with a live body with its patterned rhythms, smells, sounds, softer parts, bonier parts, body heat, breath and heart motions accompanied by my affects, along with voice tones/cadences/rhythms/content – a whole multi dimensional experience of significant-feeling present moments. Perhaps the baby could recognise in my mind my intentions to reach out to him, seek to help him, as I embodied him in my arms and words. Intentions perceived in others organise 'now moments' (Stern 2004). Simultaneously oriented to his parents' suffering, I lifted a cushion to go beneath the baby mat on the floor. I asked them if he would "shriek" before I lay him down. They said he would. He vocalised hoarsely as I stirred to move with him.

While listening to the father's monotone (affectless, exhausted) narrative, I slowly lowered the infant down without losing our whole body contact, leaning over to place him on his back on the mat. I remained bodily close to him. My hand was firmly on his middle, gently, slowly and rhythmically patting him, with little sounds to him, and within his gaze range. His mother, immobile, gazed down at him. She interrupted father's words with: "He doesn't normally look at me." I supported her in experiencing his gaze, oriented towards her, showing her how he was indeed seeking her out, to find her face, look into her eyes, in the present moment. His father said his son was thinking about food. I said he wasn't, that he was thinking about his mummy. She said, "I don't think he knows I am his mum." I tentatively suggested she come closer to him, put her head nearer, so they could see one another, a risk when intimacy can terrify. Again she said, "He does not know I'm his mum." She leaned forwards, more to his level, stroked his cheek, and looked at him. He was still looking at her, while my hand remained on his middle, regulating his states, my presence as a holding containing factor, tactile input important for brain maturation, a body-to-body form of intersubjective communication.

I placed my hands beneath the infant, tilting him, supported, to achieve eye contact with mother, patting him rhythmically to help him stay calm and alert, speaking words expressive of warmth and security through their tone and rhythm. Talking with a baby can be just as complex as gazing. I helped her think about what she might say to him. She asked him "Are you hungry?" I suggested something other than hunger. She said in descriptive impersonal form "He is adorable." I asked if she might say: "You are adorable." She came more to life as she looked directly at him and told him softly: "You are adorable, you are gorgeous, I do love you." Maternal feeling sparked in her. Imagine if you can, two women, one younger and one older, sitting close together on the floor, bending over and touching a very small person, with a growing intimacy between the three, in the presence of a witnessing father. "In the quiet moments there is no line between inner or outer but just lots of things separated out, sky seen through trees, something to do with mother's eyes all going in and out, wandering around" (Winnicott, 1948).

Retrospectively, I see my mid-wife embodiment, in the middle and between them, re-birthing this little person this time into present symbolic holding arms and minds. The infant was being bathed in gentle rhythmic up and down vocal sounds, simultaneous touch, simultaneous beholding and beheld-ness, all in a present moment. This is the kind of complete whole experience he needed to ignite his will to unfold his life and his 'intentions.' I named the struggles they had had, as the mother spoke of how her mother had looked after him, and that despite this she loves him. As the baby looked towards her eyes, I observed "He is looking at you right now." Such moments of finding the eyes of a close other person, can shift an infant's state and development, to fractally amplify self-replicating relational shapes throughout all the systems of the infant self. The mother then

suggested she was here, "So that I can become a better mummy."
Being a mummy was becoming more real. Again she said he normally
does not do this (look at her). My words were "He needs to drink
his mummy in a bit, doesn't he, hey?" The baby made little sounds.
As he gazed at her and felt her gaze at him, a moment of mutuality,
he stretched his legs, as if he felt the contact, the love, permeate his
body. Earlier chaotic yet static moments became patterned moments
with momentum. In the words of T.S. Eliot:

> But only in time can the moment in the rose garden
> The moment in the arbour where the rain beat
> The moment in the draughty church at smoke fall
> Be remembered; involved with past and future.
> The detail of the pattern is movement.

The second sequence, the baby is seven weeks old (DVD clip)

"Very in Love with Him."

This sequence from the second session constellated father, mother,
and baby as a threesome. Imagine the mother seated on the floor,
holding their baby, facing her, her arms supporting him, his eyes level
with her mouth. I suggested father come closer, come in with his wife
so "He can have both of you talking to him." Father placed his head
next to his wife's, nuzzling into her, his head against the side of her
head, together gazing intently into their child's face. How is it they
get no response from the baby, but continue their efforts? What are
they seeing in him? He is surrounded with their words, their touch,
feeling hands supporting him in that position, perhaps peripherally
aware of two persons in front of him, and I making a foursome in all.
His face seemed of wax, his eyes open, seeming not to see. Was he
hearing them, was he seeing them? And why was his mouth open? He
seemed in an un-associated state, an un-embodied state. His father
called his name twice, then "Wakey wakey," recognising his son was
as if unawakened to life, to present moments. Father looked at him
so closely, remarked on his eyelashes, mother naming them as his
daddy's eyelashes, and ears. His daddy commented humorously that
his son had his hairline (little hair) at present. He exclaimed, "Look
at his cheeks!"

Such intimate moments develop currents of Eros directed towards
and awakened within the infant, who forms in his parents' minds as
their be-loved, beloved. Stasis shifts into movement. His mother
asked why her baby wasn't calm like this at home where he often
screamed, disintegrated. His inner experience must be of opposite

poles of, a dead calm cut off state, and shrieking states. The theme of mother's love returned. I asked how it felt for her husband to have his wife in love with another. "Well, so far," he said, "I don't mind being second to him." Mother spontaneously nuzzled her baby with her nose, kissing him, her mouth on his. He blinked but remained cut off. Her husband said the baby would get upset if he nuzzled him, would cry if he kissed him. I suggested she was his mum, and he was his dad, thus naming them as separate, with different functions and ways of relating. The mother further nuzzled her son's face. "You can be a little bit physical with him, can't you?" I suggested. In that moment, all of a sudden, the baby opened his closed eyes wide, and looked as if saw his mother for the first time. But did he? It remains a question for me. His eyes seemed to not quite look at his mummy, more to the side of her. Each mouth simultaneously opened wide, a moment of mirroring, a 'moment of meeting,' a startling moment of awakening to otherness. Such shifting moments shape a new open space for the family to exist in, a new experience of time which occurs as the new state is assimilated, creating a new equilibrium. He began to cry; enough was enough. His mother moved him to her lap. In Eliot's words: "Human kind. Cannot bear very much reality."

The third sequence: the baby is nine weeks old (DVD clip)

"I've Never Seen Him This Vocal Before."

A sequence occurred two weeks later, in which the baby vocalised freely, engaging with his parents with clear eye contact. Mother, modeling and supporting how to be with them, talked with him. She said to him "You like coming here don't you. You do. You look forward to your Thursdays, yes. Yeah yeah yeah, you do. You wish you could always be like this, don't you?" The baby responded with "oho" that his mother repeated back to him. Her approach to him had become freer, as though she began to see him as a separate person with his own mind, a baby with desire to know her. Mother suggested to him that he was going to be as talkative as a child patient in the waiting room. He voiced his little thoughts throughout. It was as though he was making a developmental shift. Somewhere around eight weeks of age, writes Stern, the emergent self, from birth to two months, shifts to form a "core self"' co-existing throughout life, within later emergent aspects of a subjective self and a verbal self. I remarked on how much more focused the baby's gaze was becoming, as he looked at his mother while "talking." She found herself spontaneously kissing his hand, then saying: "Did I just kiss your hand?" I suggested she seemed to be just a little bit in love with her son. I playfully wondered aloud what her husband felt about this, her being in love with their son. He said he was becoming used to it, because early in the morning, when she comes to them, their baby will only look at her, and ignores his daddy who has cared for him all night long. The following sequence shifted to threesome interactions. Little to and fro dialogues and more circular "trialogues" arose such as:

> Baby: Hi.
> Mother: Hi, hi.
> Mother: *(to baby)* Are you saying hi, are you saying hi?
> Father: He has started this thing now C starts saying something to him and he does it back to her.
> Therapist: Oh does he!
> Mother: (to baby) Hi, hi, hi. Agoo.
> Baby: *makes varied sounds.*
> Mother: He's not normally this vocal, I've not seen him this vocal.
> Therapist: Well you just have it while it is, its lovely.
> Mother: Not this way – not this vocal, not this vocal.
> Father: It's unusual for him to be in this sort of good mood in the afternoon.

In contrast to the first sequence we saw, this baby is becoming a little person, handsome and engaging, with his own character and agency. The to and fro of turn-taking proto conversations enable the baby to feel his own capacity, to make a response happen, important for his future. "It is bodily action and reaction in relationship that are internalized to create the implicit unconscious, and this is why the extent to which the infant's agency is facilitated by the caregiver at these very early stages is so fundamental to the later psychological experience of agency" (Knox 2011). It was hard for mother to believe her baby son may desire to look at her and find her through his eyesight and mind-sight (Siegel 2010). She also found it hard to feel he really could converse with her. Perhaps the security of the setting and emotional scaffolding enabled the whole parent-infant-therapist system to relax, release tension, enable "patterns of emotional exchange" (Jacoby 1999). Sounds were expressive of feelings and intentions directed to others, experienced within the self – more fluid than future fixed words. Such moments of deintegration and reintegration are active ways of organizing and integrating experience (Fordham 1988). I then voiced: "It seems as if you have fallen in love with your mummy." The baby vociferated, their turn-taking suggesting reciprocity. I voiced how his mummy has fallen in love with him, and he with his mummy. Such embodiment moments constitute a qualitative coming together of an integration of early forming mind and body, a feeling of wholeness. The moments have a quality of movement, a quicker tempo, and livelier rhythms, along with directionality, creating connections between infant, mother, and father. Soon I suggested the father come down close to the baby too, helping him and his baby son become more closely engaged with one another, now with mother's support. They began to form an archetypal mummy, daddy baby triangle. It emerged that as mother had not known how to speak with her son, what words to say, so now her husband admitted the same. I helped him lower his voice, which was tentatively false and high, to engage his son vocally with his real deep voice, which he did. This time mother helped him with what to say. "Tell him," she said, "what you are building." The father spoke of times in the future when they would do things together, modeling the use of imagination, a basis for the infant's future imaginative capacity (Colman, 2006), dependent on good early experience. He told his son playfully that he was building the Olympic stadium, that he would take him there and he would run round it and watch football, and swim and cycle there, "Only you can't cycle yet!" The emergence of humour, signifying enjoyment, is a likely positive organizer of the infant's unrepressed unconscious.

And so we reach the end of this presentation, placing a boundary in our minds around the work with the infant and his parents, to leave them behind as we move on. Embodied moments, when imbued with truthfulness and aesthetic value, with the fire of vitality that warms the soul, with tangible kindness, that include the warmth of moments of shared enjoyment, are at the heart of Jungian analysis. They are experiences of imagination, awe and love (Gopnik, 2009), experienced in moments when body and psyche feel integrated and whole in present moments. Their fractal nature when conditions allow, may replicate their shape and qualities within the rhythms and tones, the cadences of the landscapes of a lifetime. Occasionally, moments of embodiment may have a numinous quality "felt as objective and outside the self"' (Otto, 1923, p. 11), such ineffable moments revealed 'in the emptiness of a Chinese painting or in the Incarnatus of the Credo in Bach's Mass in B Minor, the faint, whispering, lingering sequence in the fugue structure, dying away pianissimo, into a quality of numinous silence."

I end, as I began, with poetic words, from T. S. Eliot's Four Quartets:

> For most of us, there is only the unattended
> Moment, the moment in and out of time,
> The distraction fit, lost in a shaft of sunlight,
> The wild thyme unseen, or the winter lightning
> Or the waterfall, or music heard so deeply
> That it is not heard at all, but you are the music
> While the music lasts.

Bibliography

Cambray, J. (2011). Moments of complexity and enigmatic action: a Jungian view of the therapeutic field. *Journal of Analytical Psychology* (56), 290-333.

Centre, A. F. (1982). Scientific Forum on the Psychoanalytic Approach to the Nature and Location of Pathogenesis. *Bulletin of the Anna Freud Centre* (5), 87-152.

Colman, W. (2006). Imagination and the Imaginary. *Journal of Analytical Psychology, 51*(1), 21-41.

Eliot, T. S. (1945). *Four Quartets*: Faber and Faber.

Evetts-Secker, J. (2012). *At Home In The Language Of The Soul*. New Orleans: Spring Journal, Inc.

Fordham, M. (1988). The Infant's Reach. *Psychological Perspectives, 21*, 64.

Gopnik, A. (2009). *The Philosophical Baby*. London: The Bodley Head.

Hogenson, G. B. (2007). From moments of meeting to archetypal consciousness: emergence and the fractal structure of analytic practice. In A. Casement (Ed.), *Who Owns Jung?* London: Karnac.

Jacoby, M. (1999). *Jungian Psychotherapy and Contemporary Infant Research*. London: Routledge.

Jung, C. G. *Symbols and Interpretation of Dreams*. Collected Works Vol. 17 (para 543).

Jung, C. G. (1952). *Synchronicity: an Acausal Connecting Principle.* (Vol. 8).

Kalsched, D. (2013). *Trauma and the Soul*. London: Routledge.

Knox, J. (2011). *Self-Agency in Psychotherapy*. New York: W. W. Norton & Co.

MacDougal, J. (1989). *Theatres of the Body* (3rd Edition ed.). London: Free Association Books.

Nahum, J. P. (2008). Forms of Relational Meaning: Issues in the Relations Between the Implicit and Reflective-Verbal Domains: Boston Change Process Study Group. *Psychoanal. Dial., 18*(2), 125-148.

Perry, B. D., Pollard, R., Blakely, R., Baher, W., & Vigilante, D. (1995). Childhood trauma, the neurobiology of adaptation, and user-dependent development of the brain; how "states" become "traits." *Infant Mental Health Journal 16*, 271-291.

Raphael-Leff, J. (1996). Pregnancy as Procreative Process, The Placental Paradigm, And Perinatal Therapy. *J. Amer. Psychoanal. Assn., 44*, 373-399.

Stern, D. (1985). *The Interpersonal World of the Infant*. New York: Basic Books.

Stern, D. (1998). *The Motherhood Constellation: A Unified View of Parent-Infant Psychotherapy*. New York: Basic Books.

Stern, D. (2004). *The Present Moment in Psychotherapy and Everyday Life*. New York: W.W. Norton.

Wilkinson, M. (2006). *Coming into Mind*. London: Routledge.

Wilkinson, M. (2010). *Changing Minds in Therapy*. New York.

Winnicott, D. W. (1949). Mind and its relation to the psyche-soma. *British Journal of Medicine and Psychology, 27*.

Winnicott, D. W. (1958). *Collected Papers: Through Paediatrics to Psychoanalysis*. London: Tavistock.

Winnicott, D. W. (1996). Primary introduction to external reality: The early stages. In R. Shepherd, J. Johns & H. Taylor Robinson (Eds.), *Thinking about children*. London: Karnac.

Alphabetical List of Authors (in print)

Contents (CD)

Sunday, 18 August 2013

Monday, 19 August 2013

Monday Breakout Sessions

Tuesday, 20 August 2013

Tuesday Breakout Sessions

Wednesday, 21 August 2013

Thursday, 22 August 2013

Thursday Breakout Sessions

Friday, 23 August 2013

Friday Breakout Sessions

Posters

German Presentations

Author Index (CD)

IAAP CONGRESS PROCEEDINGS

MONTREAL 2010
Facing Multiplicity: Psyche, Nature, Culture
Proceedings of the 18th International Congress for Analytical Psychology
edited by Pramila Bennett
illustrated, 240 pages in print + 1789 pages on CD, ISBN 978-3-85630-744-8

CAPE TOWN 2007
Journeys, Encounters: Clinical, Communal, Cultural
Proceedings of the 17th International Congress for Analytical Psychology
edited by Pramila Bennett
illustrated, 288 pages in print + 1142 pages on CD, ISBN 978-3-85630-728-8

BARCELONA 2004
Edges of Experience: Memory and Emergence
Proceedings of the 16th International Congress for Analytical Psychology
edited by Lyn Cowan
illustrated, 240 printed pages, 1380 pages on CD, ISBN 978-3-85630-700-4

CAMBRIDGE 2001
Proceedings of the 15th International Congress for Analytical Psychology
768 pages, paperback, ISBN 978-3-85630-609-0

FLORENCE 1998: DESTRUCTION AND CREATION
Proceedings of the 14th International Congress for Analytical Psychology,
edited by Mary Ann Mattoon, 620 pages, illustrated
hardbound: ISBN 978-3-85630-584-0 / paperback: ISBN 978-3-85630-583-3

ZURICH 1995: OPEN QUESTIONS IN ANALYTICAL PSYCHOLOGY
Proceedings of the 13th International Congress for Analytical Psychology
edited by Mary Ann Mattoon
752 pages, illustrated, hardbound: ISBN 978-3-85630-555-0
paperback: ISBN 978-3-85630-556-7

CHICAGO 1992
The Transcendent Function: Individual and Collective Aspects
edited by Mary Ann Mattoon
hardbound: ISBN 978-3-85630-537-6 / paperback: ISBN 978-3-85630-538-3

PARIS 1989
Personal and Archetypal Dynamics in the Analytical Relationship.
edited by Mary Ann Mattoon
hardbound: ISBN 978-3-85630-529-1 / paperback: ISBN 978-3-85630-524-6

BERLIN 1986
The Archetype of Shadow in a Split World
edited by Mary Ann Mattoon
The 10th International Congress of Analytical Psychology was held in Berlin,
September 2 – 9, 1986. 456 pages, numerous illustrations and diagrams
hardbound: ISBN 978-3-85630-514-7 / paperback: ISBN 978-3-85630-506-2

JERUSALEM 1983
Symbolic and Clinical Approaches in Theory and Practice
edited by Luigi Zoja and Robert Hinshaw
This handsome volume, drawn from the 9th International Congress of Analytical Psychology in Jerusalem, contains contributions reflecting on the
meaning and significance of contemporary analytical work from 25 prominent
Jungian analysts from around the world.
375 pages, hardbound, illustrated, ISBN 978-3-85630-504-8

Montreal 2010

Facing Multiplicity: Psyche, Nature, Culture

edited by Pramila Bennett

Jungian analysts from all over the world gathered in Montreal from August 22 to 27, 2010.

The 11 plenary presentations and the 100 break-out sessions attest to the complex dynamics and dilemmas facing the community in present-day culture. The Pre-Congress Workshop on Movement as Active Imagination papers are also recorded. There is a foreword by Tom Kelly with the opening address of Joe Cambray and the farewell address of Hester Solomon. The plenary presentations are printed in this volume and a CD with all of the Congress presentations (180 altogether) and numerous illustrations can be found inside the back cover.

(240 pages in print, paperback + 1789 pages on CD with numerous color illustrations, ISBN 978-3-85630-744-8)

Montreal 2010
Facing Multiplicity: Psyche, Nature, Culture

Proceedings of the XVIIIth Congress of the International Association for Analytical Psychology

Edited by Pramila Bennett

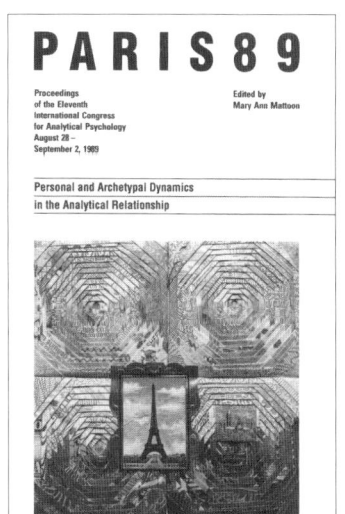

PARIS 89

Proceedings of the Eleventh International Congress for Analytical Psychology August 28 – September 2, 1989

Edited by Mary Ann Mattoon

Personal and Archetypal Dynamics in the Analytical Relationship

Paris 1989

Dynamics in Relationship

edited by Mary Ann Mattoon

The 11th International Congress for Analytical Psychology was held in Paris from August 28 through September 2, 1989. It is no surprise that the theme of "Personal and Archetypal Dynamics in the Analytical Relationship" succeeded in drawing widely varying and controversial responses. More than ever before the fifty-five contributors of papers represent Jungian groups from around the globe in every sense. However, while differences of approach are evident throughout this fascinating collection, so too is an ever more significant sense of synthesis: in the end we all share a common task.

510 pages, illustrated
ISBN 978-3-85630-529-1 (Hardcover) 978-3-85630-524-6 (Paperback)

ENGLISH TITLES FROM DAIMON

R. Abt / I. Bosch / V. MacKrell - *Dream Child, Creation and New Life
in Dreams of Pregnant Women*
Ruth Ammann - *The Enchantment of Gardens*
Susan R. Bach - *Life Paints its Own Span*
Diana Baynes Jansen – *Jung's Apprentice: A Biography of Helton Godwin Baynes*
John Beebe (Ed.) - *Terror, Violence and the Impulse to Destroy*
E.A. Bennet - *Meetings with Jung*
W.H. Bleek / L.C. Lloyd (Ed.) - *Specimens of Bushman Folklore*
Tess Castleman - *Threads, Knots, Tapestries*
- *Sacred Dream Circles*
Heinrich Karl Fierz - *Jungian Psychiatry*
John Fraim - *Battle of Symbols*
von Franz / Frey-Rohn / Jaffé - *What is Death?*
Liliane Frey-Rohn - *Friedrich Nietzsche, A Psychological Approach*
Marion Gallbach - *Learning from Dreams*
Ralph Goldstein (Ed.) - *Images, Meanings and Connections:
Essays in Memory of Susan Bach*
Yael Haft - *Hands: Archetypal Chirology*
Fred Gustafson - *The Black Madonna of Einsiedeln*
Daniel Hell - *Soul-Hunger: The Feeling Human Being and the Life-Sciences*
Siegmund Hurwitz - *Lilith, the first Eve*
Aniela Jaffé - *The Myth of Meaning*
- *Was C.G. Jung a Mystic?*
- *From the Life und Work of C.G. Jung*
- *Death Dreams and Ghosts*
Verena Kast - *A Time to Mourn*
- *Sisyphus*
Hayao Kawai - *Dreams, Myths and Fairy Tales in Japan*
James Kirsch - *The Reluctant Prophet*
Eva Langley-Dános - *Prison on Wheels: Ravensbrück to Burgau*
Mary Lynn Kittelson - *Sounding the Soul*
Rivkah Schärf Kluger - *The Gilgamesh Epic*
Yehezkel Kluger & - *RUTH in the Light of Mythology, Legend*
Naomi Kluger-Nash *and Kabbalah*
Paul Kugler (Ed.) - *Jungian Perspectives on Clinical Supervision*
Paul Kugler - *The Alchemy of Discourse*
Rafael López-Pedraza - *Cultural Anxiety*
- *Hermes and his Children*
Alan McGlashan - *The Savage and Beautiful Country*
- *Gravity and Levity*
Gregory McNamee (Ed.) - *The Girl Who Made Stars: Bushman Folklore*
- *The Bearskin Quiver*
- *The North Wind and the Sun & Other Fables of Aesop*
Gitta Mallasz - *Talking with Angels*
C.A. Meier - *Healing Dream and Ritual*
- *A Testament to the Wilderness*
- *Personality: The Individuation Process*
Eva Pattis Zoja (Ed.) - *Sandplay Therapy*
Laurens van der Post - *The Rock Rabbit and the Rainbow*

ENGLISH TITLES FROM DAIMON